# Table of Contents

# Top 15 Test Taking Tips

1. Know the test directions, duration, topics, question types, how many questions

2. Setup a flexible study schedule at least 3-4 weeks before test day

3. Study during the time of day you are most alert, relaxed, and stress free

4. Maximize your learning style; visual learner use visual study aids, auditory learner use auditory study aids

5. Focus on your weakest knowledge base

6. Find a study partner to review with and help clarify questions

7. Practice, practice, practice

8. Get a good night's sleep; don't try to cram the night before the test

9. Eat a well balanced meal

10. Wear comfortable, loose fitting, layered clothing; prepare for it to be either cold or hot during the test

11. Eliminate the obviously wrong answer choices, then guess the first remaining choice

12. Pace yourself; don't rush, but keep working and move on if you get stuck

13. Maintain a positive attitude even if the test is going poorly

14. Keep your first answer unless you are positive it is wrong

15. Check your work, don't make a careless mistake

# Reading: Informational Texts

*Read the following passage, and then choose the best answer for each question.*

## All About Corn

Corn is a grain. People and animals eat it for food. Corn is raised on farms, in big fields. The plants are called stalks. Stalks of corn can grow very tall. Many times they are over six feet tall. That is taller than most human beings. The part of the stalk that has the corn is called an ear.

Most ears of corn are yellow. Some are white. Corn has many uses. Most corn is used to feed animals, such as cows and pigs. Some of it is sold to food companies, and is used as food for people. This is where we get canned corn, and corn on the cob. It is also used in corn bread and popcorn.

**1. Where does corn grow?**

a. In stores
b. In the ocean
c. On farms
d. In the forest

**2. What are corn plants called?**

a. Zones
b. Eggs
c. Trees
d. Stalks

**3. Stalks of corn are very ______.**

a. Wide
b. Tall
c. Heavy
d. Short

**4. What do we call the part of the stalk that has the corn?**

a. A leg
b. A twig
c. An ear
d. A stick

*Read the following passage, and then choose the best answer for each question.*

## All About Birds

Birds fly in the air. They can fly because they have wings. Birds come in lots of sizes. Some are big birds, and some are small birds. They come in all kinds of colors, too. Some are red. Some are blue. Many are black. A lot of birds are brown.

Most birds live in trees. They make a nest for a home. They use twigs and leaves to make a nest. They lay eggs in the nest. Baby birds come from eggs. After baby birds hatch, their mom and dad feed them with worms and bugs and seeds. After baby birds grow up, they move out. Then they make their own nest, and start a new family.

**1. Where do most birds live?**

a. In barns
b. In cages
c. In lakes
d. In trees

**2. Why can birds fly?**

a. Because they have wings
b. Because they are little
c. Because they are brown
d. Because they have beaks

**3. What is a food a baby bird eats?**

a. Apples
b. Worms
c. Hot dogs
d. Oatmeal

**4. What is one kind of thing a nest is made of?**

a. Glue
b. Leaves
c. Eggs
d. Nails

*Read the following passage, and then choose the best answer for each question.*

## Ronald Reagan

Ronald Reagan was born over a hundred years ago, on February 6th, 1911. He was raised in the small town of Dixon, Illinois. In high school, he had a job as a lifeguard on Rock River. A lifeguard is a person who rescues people who are drowning. Ronald Reagan saved 77 people from drowning.

He went to college in the same state where he grew up. After college he moved to Iowa, which is right next to Illinois. His first job there was at a radio station. Then he moved to Hollywood and became an actor. In one of his most famous movies he worked with a chimpanzee. It was called Bedtime For Bonzo.

During World War II, Ronald Reagan joined the Air Force. Back then it was called the Army Air Force. After the war was over, he started appearing on TV shows. He began making speeches about the government, too. Many people liked his speeches. Soon, people began asking Ronald Reagan to run for President. At first he didn't want to. He wanted to start in a less important job. So he ran for Governor of the state of California, and he won. He was Governor of California from 1967 to 1975. Several years later, in 1980, he ran for President, and he won. He defeated Jimmy Carter, who was the President at the time. Ronald Reagan served as President of the United States from 1981 to 1989.

**1. What would be another good title for this text?**

a. Chimpanzees Are Funny
b. Presidents and Movies
c. Life In A Small Town
d. The Ronald Reagan Story

**2. Ronald Reagan went to college in which state?**

a. Ohio
b. California
c. Illinois
d. Texas

**3. What do you call someone who has a job rescuing people from drowning?**

a. Saver
b. Beach helper
c. Police officer
d. Lifeguard

**4. How many people did Ronald Reagan save from drowning?**

a. 77
b. 22
c. 11
d. 5

**5. Where was Ronald Reagan's first job after college?**

a. At a radio station
b. At a grocery store
c. At a bank
d. In the Air Force

**6. What does it mean when it says Ronald Reagan defeated Jimmy Carter?**

a. It means he gave Jimmy Carter a gift.
b. It means he was taller than Jimmy Carter.
c. It means he got more votes than Jimmy Carter and won the election for President.
d. It means he said something about Jimmy Carter that wasn't very nice.

**7. Which state elected Ronald Reagan as Governor?**

a. Ohio
b. Illinois
c. California
d. Texas

**8. What job did Ronald Reagan hold in 1983?**

a. President of the United States
b. Police officer
c. Lifeguard
d. Banker

*Read the following passage, and then choose the best answer for each question.*

## Molly's Chores

Molly is only seven years old, but she is a big help on her parents' farm.

She has chores to do every day. She sweeps the kitchen floor every night. She feeds the pigs, too.

She fills the water bin for the family cow.

She also helps take care of her little brothers.

Molly loves her family and her farm. She is glad to help.

**1a. How old is Molly? Circle your answer below.**

3 5 7 9

**1b. Did you learn this from the words or from the pictures? Circle your answer below.**

Words Pictures

**2a. How many brothers does Molly have?**

1 2 3 4

**2b. Did you learn this from the words or from the pictures? Circle your answer below.**

Words Pictures

**3a. What chore does Molly do in the kitchen?**

Sweep Mop Cook Fold

**3b. Did you learn this from the words or from the pictures? Circle your answer below.**

Words Pictures

**4a. How many pigs are on the farm?**

2 3 4 5

**4b. Did you learn this from the words or from the pictures? Circle your answer below.**

Words Pictures

**5a. Is there a barn on Molly's farm?**

Yes No

**5b. Did you learn this from the words or from the pictures? Circle your answer below.**

Words Pictures

*Read the following, and then draw a line between the state and the picture that goes with the state.*

## 50 Different States

Look at a map of the United States of America. It is big; there are 50 states in the country. In some ways, states are a lot alike. In other ways, they are different. Some states have mild weather most of the year, like California. Other states, like Texas, can be very hot in the summer. Some states are mostly flat. Some states, like Utah, have mountains where people ski. Then there is the Grand Canyon. It's in Arizona. Different things grow better in different states. Kansas is famous for growing lots of wheat. Florida is famous for growing oranges. These are just a few of the differences in our 50 great states.

1. Kansas
2. Florida
3. Arizona
4. Utah
5. Texas

*Read the following passage, and then choose the best answer for each question.*

## The Big Game

by Jose Ramirez

Dad is taking me to the Cubs baseball game tomorrow. Dad usually drives, but his car is in the shop. We will probably take the bus. I think the Cubs will win, because they have won five games in a row. I hope it doesn't rain. If it rains the game will be called off. I don't think it is going to rain. It isn't cloudy today. I think we'll have good seats because Dad said the tickets cost a lot of money. I love the hot dogs at the stadium, but I have to be careful. Last time I had two hot dogs, and I got sick. Dad will probably only buy me one hot dog at this game. That's OK, though. I'm just happy we're going to see the game. I love the Cubs.

**1. Why does Jose think he and his Dad will take the bus?**

a. The bus is cheaper than driving.
b. The bus is faster than driving.
c. His dad can't find his driver's license.
d. His dad's car is getting repaired.

**2. Why does Jose think it won't rain the next day?**

a. His dad said so.
b. It isn't cloudy.
c. His friend said so.
d. He heard it on the weather report.

**3. Why does Jose think the seats will be good?**

a. Because they cost a lot of money.
b. Because he and his dad sat in those seats last time.
c. Because the tickets are blue.
d. Because a friend said so.

**4. Why does Jose think the Cubs will win tomorrow?**

a. He feels lucky.
b. The Cubs have won several games in a row.
c. The Cubs have a new pitcher.
d. The Cubs are his favorite team.

**5. Why did Jose get sick the last time he went to a Cubs game?**

a. It was cold and rainy.
b. He ate too much.
c. He got stung by a bee.
d. He got sun stroke.

*Read the following passage, and then choose the best answer for each question.*

## What's Different? What's the Same?

Shelley lives in a small town. She is six year old. She has a brother, and she walks to school with him every day. Shelley likes reading and playing soccer after school. She wants to be a nurse when she grows up.

Andre is six years old. He lives in a very big city. He has a brother and a sister, and every day they walk to school. Andre likes playing soccer after school. He also likes to fly kites and ride bikes. He wants to be a lawyer when he grows up.

**1. Who lives in a small town?**

a. Shelley
b. Andre
c. Both

**2. Who has a sister?**

a. Shelley
b. Andre
c. Both

**3. Who likes flying kites?**

a. Shelley
b. Andre
c. Both

**4. Who has a brother?**

a. Shelley
b. Andre
c. Both

**5. Who walks to school?**

a. Shelley
b. Andre
c. Both

**6. Who has a sister?**

a. Shelley
b. Andre
c. Both

**7. Who wants to become a lawyer?**

a. Shelley
b. Andre
c. Both

**8. Who likes playing soccer?**

a. Shelley
b. Andre
c. Both

# Reading: Literature

*Read the following passage, and then choose the best answer for each question.*

## Billy and His Brother

Billy and his Dad were in their living room. They were sitting on a couch. They were watching TV. Billy's cat was sleeping in a chair.

Then Billy's brother came in. He wanted to watch TV, too. So he put the cat on the floor. Then he sat in the chair. The cat walked into the kitchen.

**1. What room was Billy in?**

a. kitchen
b. bedroom
c. living room
d. dining room

**2. Where was Billy sitting?**

a. on the couch
b. on the floor
c. on a chair
d. on the steps

**3. Where was Billy's cat?**

a. on the couch
b. on top of the TV
c. on the chair
d. on the stairs

**4. Why did Billy's brother move the cat?**

a. he was just playing
b. he wanted to feed him
c. he doesn't like cats
d. he wanted to sit in the chair

*Read the following passage, and then choose the best answer for each question.*

## Cindy in the Kitchen

Cindy was helping her mom make cookies for the first time. Helping in the kitchen made Cindy feel like a big girl.

Her mom let Cindy do most of the work. She also watched her carefully. She wanted to make sure Cindy didn't make any mistakes.

"Careful, dear! Don't put in too much milk. We want to make oatmeal cookies, not oatmeal soup!"

Cindy giggled. She was glad her mom was there to help her.

In a little while the cookies were all done, hot and fresh from the oven. Cindy and her mom had milk and cookies for a snack. Then her mom put the rest of the cookies in a cookie jar.

**1. Why did Cindy like helping in the kitchen?**

a. it was warm in the kitchen
b. it smelled good in there
c. it made her feel like a big girl
d. she got extra snacks for helping

**2. Cindy almost put too much _________ in the cookie dough.**

a. butter
b. milk
c. salt
d. sugar

**3. How often does Cindy help her mom make cookies?**

a. every day
b. once a week
c. this was her first time ever
d. once a month

**4. What happened to the leftover cookies?**

a. Cindy's mom put them in a cookie jar
b. Cindy's brother ate them
c. they got thrown away
d. Cindy gave them to a friend

**5. What would be a good title for this story?**

a. Cookies Taste Good
b. The Kitchen Is Big
c. Cindy Goes To School
d. Cindy Helps Mom In The Kitchen

**6. What did Cindy's mom mean when she said they weren't making soup?**

a. they would have soup later
b. she doesn't like soup
c. oatmeal soup is her favorite
d. too much milk would make the cookie mix runny like soup

*Read the following passage, and then choose the best answer for each question.*

## Mr. Smith and the Garden

Mr. Smith went to the store.

He bought some seeds.

He bought lettuce seeds, and carrot seeds.

Then he planted the seeds in his garden.

The garden is in his back yard.

Soon the seeds will start growing.

Plants will come up from the ground.

Every day Mr. Smith will take care of the plants.

When they are grown, Mr. Smith will pick them.

Then he will eat them in salads.

**1. What would be another good title for this story?**

a. Summertime Is Fun
b. I Like Lettuce
c. Mr. Smith Plants Some Seeds
d. All About Carrots

**2. Where did Mr. Smith get his seeds?**

a. from his wife
b. from his neighbor
c. he found them
d. from the store

**3. What kind of seeds did Mr. Smith plant?**

a. carrot and tomato
b. carrot and lettuce
c. lettuce and turnip
d. lettuce and tomato

**4. After Mr. Smith picks the carrots and lettuce, what will he do with them?**

a. eat them
b. feed them to his pet rabbit
c. freeze them
d. give them away

*Read the following passage, and then choose the best answer for each question.*

## Pedro and the Zoo

Pedro's dad said "Let's go the zoo." Pedro jumped up and down and cheered: "Yay! We are going to the zoo!" Then his mom told him he had to clean his room before they could leave. Pedro said "That's not fair! I want to go right now!" His dad told him "Your mom is right. Chores come before fun." He said they would go to the zoo after Pedro cleaned his room. So Pedro cleaned his room. As soon as he did, he and his mom and dad went to the zoo. Pedro was glad he cleaned his room.

**1. How did Pedro feel when his dad said "let's go to the zoo"?**

a. he was mad
b. he was sad
c. he was happy
d. he didn't care

**2. How did Pedro feel when his mom told him to clean his room?**

a. he was mad
b. he was sad
c. he was happy
d. he didn't care

**3. Why was Pedro glad he cleaned his room?**

a. because his mom baked him a cake
b. because he got to go to the zoo
c. because his dad hugged him
d. because he found his lost toy

**4. A good title for this story would be**

a. Pedro and The Animals
b. Pedro and His Sister
c. Fun at The Park
d. A Lesson for Pedro

**5. Who said "chores come before fun"?**

a. Pedro
b. Pedro's mom
c. nobody said that
d. Pedro's dad

*Read the following passage, and then choose the best answer for each question.*

## Ashley and the Circus

Ashley giggled at the clowns.

They looked funny.

They came out of a tiny car.

Then she clapped for the lion tamer.

His lion did a lot of tricks.

Ashley was glad her parents brought her.

She was also glad when it was time to go home.

She was tired.

It was past her bedtime.

She fell asleep on the way home.

**1. Where did this story take place?**

a. at school
b. at home
c. at a circus
d. at a store

**2. What time did this story take place?**

a. morning
b. noon
c. afternoon
d. at night

**3. How do you know where the story took place?**

a. Ashley said so
b. there were clowns and a lion tamer
c. Ashley giggled
d. Ashley's mom said so

**4. How do you know when the story took place?**

a. it was past Ashley's bedtime
b. it was dark
c. Ashley said so
d. a clown said so

*Read the following, and then write the best answer in the blank for each question based off the story.*

## Ray's Story

Ray has a new bike.

Ray has a pet.

Ray has nice sisters.

Ray saves his money.

Ray is happy.

1. Ray's bike is ________________________.
2. Ray's has a pet ________________________.
3. How many sisters does Ray have? ________________________
4. Ray saves his money in a ________________________ ________________________.
5. Ray is smiling because he is ________________________.

*Read the following passage, and then number the pictures in the correct order based on the story.*

## Emma's Day Off

Emma rubbed her eyes. Was it morning already? It seemed as if she had just gone to sleep. She got out of bed. It was time to get ready for school. She went into the kitchen to eat breakfast. Her mom was there. Emma's mom said that today was a special day because school had been canceled. Emma asked why there was no school. Her mom told her to look outside. Emma ran to the window and couldn't believe her eyes. "There must be a foot of snow, Mom! Oh, boy, a snow day!" Her mother smiled. "Let's make pancakes, and then we'll go sledding, Emma." So, after breakfast, Emma and her mom went sledding. Then they made a snowman. Emma had fun on her day off.

1. ________

2. Zzzz... ________

3. ________

4. ________

5. ________

# Reading: Foundational Skills

## Long and Short Vowels

### Long A and Short A

For each question below, write the word the picture represents. Then circle whether the vowel is long or short.

1. What is the word? ________________ Long Short

2. What is the word? ________________ Long Short

3. What is the word? ________________ Long Short

4. What is the word? ________________ Long Short

5. What is the word? ________________ Long Short

## Long E and Short E

For each question below, write the word the picture represents. Then circle whether the vowel is long or short.

1. What is the word? ____________ Long Short

2. What is the word? ____________ Long Short

3. What is the word? ____________ Long Short

4. What is the word? ____________ Long Short

5. What is the word? ____________ Long Short

## Long I and Short I

For each question below, write the word the picture represents. Then circle whether the vowel is long or short.

1.  What is the word? ______________ Long Short

2.  What is the word? ______________ Long Short

3.  What is the word? ______________ Long Short

4.  What is the word? ______________ Long Short

5.  What is the word? ______________ Long Short

## Long O and Short O

For each question below, write the word the picture represents. Then circle whether the vowel is long or short.

1.  What is the word? ____________ Long Short

2.  What is the word? ____________ Long Short

3.  What is the word? ____________ Long Short

4.  What is the word? ____________ Long Short

5. 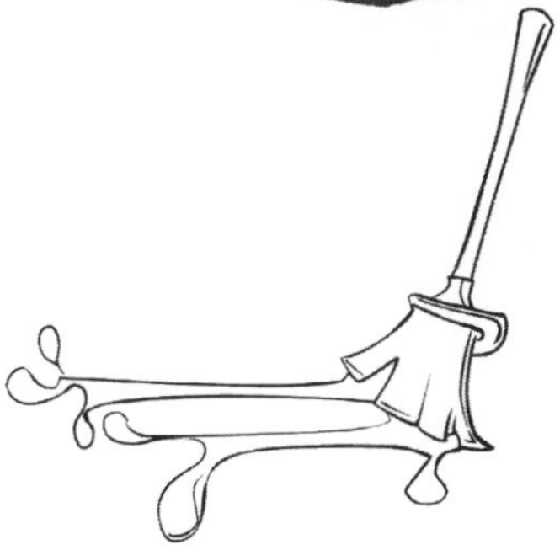 What is the word? ____________ Long Short

## Long U and Short U

For each question below, write the word the picture represents. Then circle whether the vowel is long or short.

1. 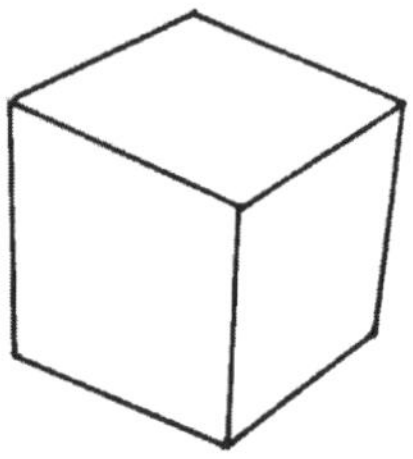 What is the word? ______________ Long Short

2. 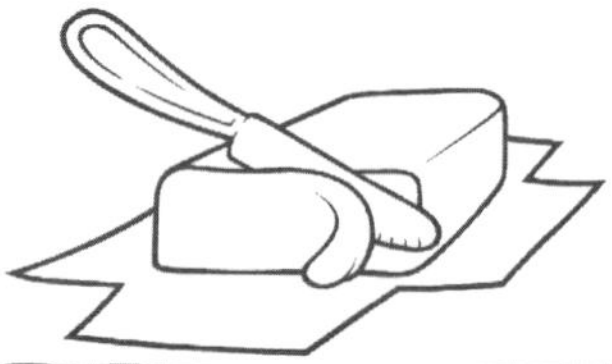 What is the word? ______________ Long Short

3. 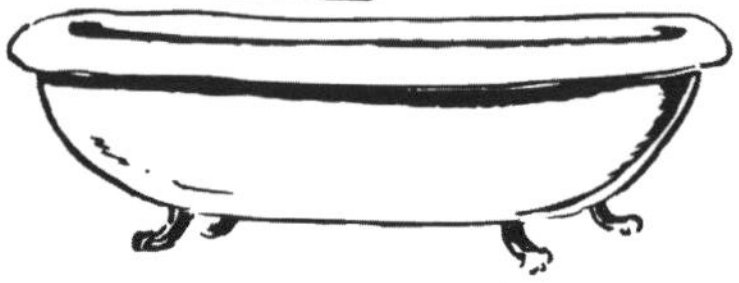 What is the word? ______________ Long Short

4.  What is the word? ______________ Long Short

5.  What is the word? ______________ Long Short

# Consonant Blends and Digraphs

**BL, BR, FL, FR**

Fill in the blank with the word that matches the picture. Each answer should start with bl, br, fl, or fr.

1. The flag is red, white and ____________.

2. The bowling ball is ____________.

3. A rose is a pretty ____________.

4. Birds ____________ through the air.

5. People ____________ when they are sad.

6. I like butter on my ____________.

7. I use my ____________ when I think.

8. The rubber duck is ____________ on the water.

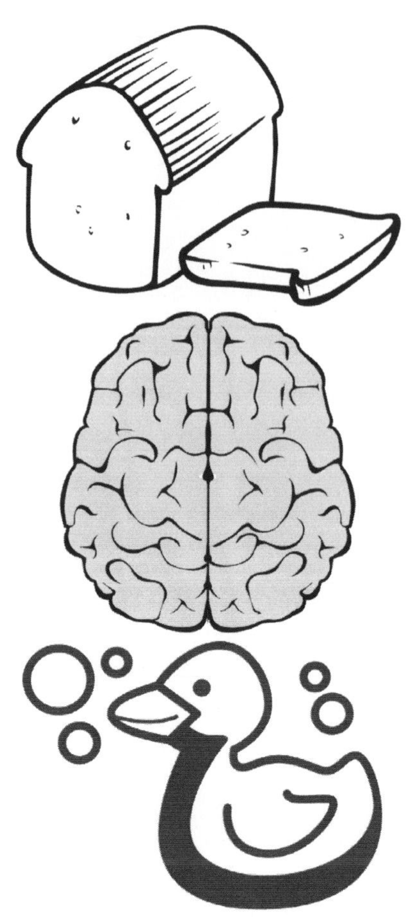

**CL, CR, CH, WH**

Fill in the blank with the word that matches the picture. Each answer should start with cl, cr, ch, or wh.

1. The snowman is ____________.

2. We go to ____________ every Sunday.

3. The king is wearing a ____________ on his head.

4. The alarm ____________ is very loud.

5. The ____________ at the circus made me laugh.

6. Always look both ways before you ____________ the street.

7. I like potato ____________ for a snack.

8. I saw a ____________ at Sea World last year.

**GL, PL, SL**

Fill in the blank with the word that matches the picture. Each answer should start with gl, pl, or sl.

1. Going down the ______________ is my favorite part of recess.

2. The ______________ keeps the water from going down the drain.

3. My ______________ matches my cup and saucer.

4. In winter, ______________ keep my hands warm.

5. My teacher has a ______________ that shows all the different countries.

6. When it snows I will try out my new ______________.

**TH, TR, GR**

Fill in the blank with the word that matches the picture. Each answer should start with th, tr, or gr.

1. A ____________ whistle is very loud.

2. Mom bought apples and ____________ at the store.

3. My cat likes to climb the ____________ in our front yard.

4. I like ____________ on my mashed potatoes.

5. A hand has four fingers and a ____________.

6. Ten plus ten plus ten equals ____________.

**SH, SK, ST**

Fill in the blank with the word that matches the picture. Each answer should start with sh, sk, or st.

1. I have a new pair of ____________.

2. We get wool from ____________.

3. When the pond freezes, we go ice ____________.

4. I like to lay on the grass and look up at the ____________.

5. Last night we had ____________ for dinner.

6. There are 50 ____________ in the USA.

**SM, SN, SP**

Fill in the blank with the word that matches the picture. Each answer should start with sm, sn, or sp.

1. We ____________ when we are happy.

2. A ____________ doesn't move very fast.

3. I don't like spiders or ____________.

4. Dalmatians have a lot of ____________.

5. I used a ____________ to wash the dishes.

**SH, -CH, -ND, -CK**

Fill in the blank with the word that matches the picture. Each answer should end with sh, ch, nd, or ck.

1. Always ____________ your hands before eating.

2. Fish and frogs can live in a ____________.

3. My brother and I made a ____________ castle at the beach.

4. I brought an egg sandwich for my ____________.

5. A ____________ has webbed feet and quacks.

6. My uncle has a job driving a ____________.

7. Sammy got a new ____________ for his birthday.

8. ____________ live in the water.

**-NT, -MP, -NK, -ST**

Fill in the blank with the word that matches the picture. Each answer should end with nt, mp, nk, or st.

1. An ____________ is an insect you don't want at picnics.

2. Every letter must have a ____________ on it.

3. I save money in a piggy ____________.

4. A bird will build a ____________ for a home.

5. Watch out for the ____________!

6. I turned on the ____________ so I could see better.

7. I had eggs and ____________ for breakfast.

8. We are going to camp out in a ____________.

# Rhymes

## What Rhymes With It?

Draw a line from the word on the left to the word that rhymes with it.

| | |
|---|---|
| 1. Bat | Dog |
| 2. Frog | Rope |
| 3. More | Cat |
| 4. Far | Car |
| 5. Soap | Store |

# Spelling

## What Is It?

Look at each picture, and then write what it is in the blank below it.

1.

____________________

2.

____________________

3.

____________________

4.

____________________

5.

____________________

6.

____________________

7.

____________________

8.

____________________

9.

____________________

# Another Look at Long Vowels

## Words That End With an E

Many words with long vowels end with an e. Here are some pictures. Look at each one, and then spell the word that fits with the picture, with a long vowel word that ends with an e.

1. I use a ____________ to wash the car.

2. I ____________ the bus to school yesterday.

3. Let's ____________ some cookies!

4. Every ____________ of snow is different.

5. We say ____________ before every meal.

6. When the apples are ____________ we will pick them.

7. I like peanut butter and ____________ jelly.

8. Dad helped me learn to ride a ___________.

9. The final ___________ of the baseball game was 3-0.

10. Our ___________ bush is blooming.

## Common Long Vowel Combinations

Next to each picture, there is a sentence. Each sentence has part of a word missing. Fill in the blank with the vowel combination that completes the word, based on the picture.

1. C_______l comes from mines that go deep in the ground.

2. My f______t are getting so big I need new shoes.

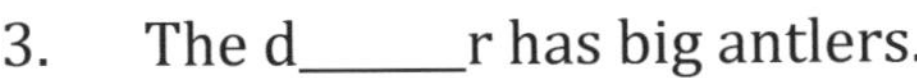

3. The d______r has big antlers.

4. I'm so hungry I could _______t a horse!

5. It's so quiet you can hear a mouse squ_______k.

6. I can t______ my own shoes.

7. My dad wears a s______t to work every day.

8. Eating fr_______t is tasty and healthy.

9. It's r_______ning, so let's stay inside.

10. This weekend we are going to p_______nt my room.

# Syllables

## How Many Syllables?

Look at each picture. Then look at the name of the object next to the picture. Then circle the number of syllables in the name of the object. Remember, every syllable has to have a vowel sound.

1. frog

1 2 3 4

2. house

1 2 3 4

3. pony

1 2 3 4

4. elephant

1 2 3 4

5. cat

1 2 3 4

6. teacher

1 2 3 4

7. basketball

1 2 3 4

8. strawberry

1 2 3 4

9. airplane

1 2 3 4

10.  dog

1 2 3 4

## Let's Break It Up!

Look at the name of each object pictured. The name of each one has two syllables. On the blank line, divide the word into two syllables, with a space between each syllable.

1. ________________ ________________

mailman

2. ________________ ________________

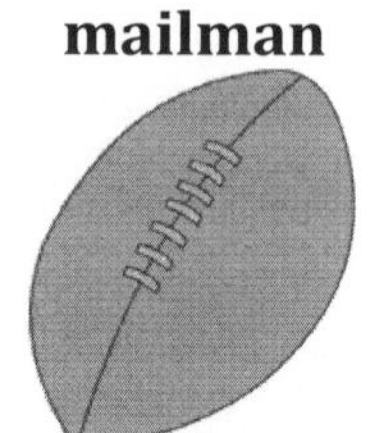

football

3. ________________ ________________

hammer

4. ________________ ________________

oven

5. ________________ ________________

raining

6. ________________ ________________

problem

7. ____________________ ____________________

money

8. ____________________ ____________________

woman

9. ____________________ ____________________

city

10. ____________________ ____________________

seven

# Comprehension and Recognition

## Sentence Comprehension

Read each sentence. Then choose the answer that finishes or matches each sentence.

**1. Students ride in this to school.**

a.

b.

c.

d.

**2. This likes water and it quacks.**

a.

b.

c.

d.

**3. This is a _______.**

a. puppy
b. airplane
c. cloud
d. house

### WORD RECOGNITION

In each question below, part of the word is underlined. Pick the answer whose word has the same sound that the underlined part makes.

**1. pan**

a. fog
b. puppy
c. kite
d. ball

**2. flower**

a. cow
b. dog
c. sled
d. sun

**3. flew**

a. new
b. sand
c. time
d. string

**4. fry**

a. town
b. hill
c. frown
d. duck

## Identifying Sounds at the Beginning of Words

Each question has a drawing, and the name of what is in the drawing. Read the name of the item in the picture out loud. Then pick the word that starts with the same sound as the item.

**1. car**

a. cat
b. bread
c. worm
d. clown

**2. duck**

a. horse
b. bike
c. dog
d. tooth

**3. toes**

a. school
b. church
c. smile
d. top

**4. moon**

a. up
b. over
c. move
d. cat

# Reading: Language

## Nouns

A noun is a person, place or thing. Words like cat, bell, brownie, joy, doctor, holiday, car, teacher, lake, bus, finger, snow, and sadness are nouns.

Each of these problems has three words. One of the words is a noun. Circle the word that is a noun.

| | | | |
|---|---|---|---|
| 1. | red | rusty | rope |
| 2. | lake | blue | big |
| 3. | slow | brown | turtle |
| 4. | fast | car | drove |
| 5. | book | long | funny |
| 6. | hat | think | jump |
| 7. | like | face | had |
| 8. | tall | fruit | up |
| 9. | wide | long | dime |
| 10. | skinny | short | ball |

## Proper Nouns

A proper noun is a particular person, place or thing. Words and phrases like *Dad, Mrs. Brooks, Atlantic Ocean, Doctor Brown, America, Canada, Jupiter, Christmas, President Lincoln,* and *South Dakota* are proper nouns. Proper nouns should always start with capital letters.

Each line has three words or phrases. One of them is a proper noun. Circle the word or phrase that is a proper noun.

| | | | |
|---|---|---|---|
| 1. | car | jump | Jane |
| 2. | Mr. Martinez | soap | blue |
| 3. | fast | read | President Obama |
| 4. | run | drink | Empire State Building |
| 5. | water | moon | Grandpa |
| 6. | town | Doctor Harris | hospital |
| 7. | Smoky Bear | wolf | park |
| 8. | Atlanta Braves | team | baseball |
| 9. | summer | winter | Easter |
| 10. | dog | cat | Fluffy |

# Possessive Nouns

A possessive noun is a noun that shows that a thing belongs to something or someone. Possessive nouns make it easier to say and write many things. Instead of always saying *the ball that belongs to Tommy*, we say *Tommy's ball*. Instead of always saying *the puppy that belongs to Cindy*, we say *Cindy's puppy*.

That little mark before the *s* at the end of the words is called an apostrophe. Possessive nouns always have an apostrophe, and they usually end in the letter *s*, too.

All nouns can be possessive, not just the names of people. Here are some examples:

*The town's mayor is a lawyer.*

*The ball's colors are very bright.*

*The teacher talked to the school's students.*

To show that something belongs to only one person or thing, you should use an apostrophe and *s* to make the possessive noun. Like these:

*The cat's paws are clean*

*You should listen to your father's advice.*

*Your sister's new shoes are nice and shiny.*

To show that something belongs to more than one person or thing, you should also use an apostrophe and *s*, unless the word ends in *s*. Then you can just use an apostrophe. Like these:

*The cars' horns were very loud.*

*We need to clean the horses' stalls.*

*Roses' thorns are very sharp.*

Each of the following problems shows something that belongs to something or someone, or more than one person or thing. Read each one, and then choose the answer that shows the correct possessive noun form.

**1. the baseball bat of Billy**

a. Billys' baseball bat
b. Billy's baseball bat
c. Billys baseball bat

**2. the food dishes of the cats**

a. the cats' food dishes
b. the cats's food dishes
c. the cats food dishes

**3. the car that belongs to my dad**

a. my dad's car
b. my dads car
c. my dads' car

**4. the house of my grandparents**

a. my grandparents house
b. my grandparents' house
c. my grandparent's house

**5. the noise of the blender**

a. the blenders noise
b. the blenders' noise
c. the blender's noise

**6. the aroma of the flowers**

a. the flowers' aroma
b. the flowers aroma'
c. the flowers's aroma

**7. the sister of my friend**

a. my friend's sister
b. my friends' sister
c. my friends sister'

**8. the sisters of my friends**

a. my friends sisters
b. my friends's sisters'
c. my friends' sisters

**9. the collar that my dog wears**

a. my dogs collar
b. my dogs' collar
c. my dog's collar

**10. the desk of the teacher**

a. the teachers desk
b. the teachers' desk
c. the teacher's desk

## Personal Pronouns

We use pronouns every day. Pronouns are words that refer to a person, place or thing, but not by their names.

*Personal pronouns* are words that we use in place of names of a person, place or thing. Words like *I, me, you, they, them, we, us, he, her, him, it* and *she* are personal pronouns. Look at this passage:

*I picked the puppy up. The puppy was happy. The puppy wagged his tail and then the puppy licked my face.*

That sounds strange, because we keep saying "the puppy" over and over. Let's use pronouns to make it sound better:

*I picked the puppy up. He was happy. He wagged his tail and then he licked my face.*

Doesn't that sound better?

Now you can practice using pronouns. First, look at these sentences. Each one has a pronoun. Pick the answer that shows the pronoun.

**1. He threw the ball to Toni.**

a. Toni
b. ball
c. He
d. threw

**2. They will be here later.**

a. They
b. be
c. here
d. later

**3. Mike said he didn't want any more milk.**

a. milk
b. Mike
c. want
d. he

**4. Mom said I can stay up late.**

a. said
b. I
c. Mom
d. late

**5. Mrs. Smith thinks it is going to rain.**

a. think
b. rain
c. going
d. it

**6. Share your toys with him, Joe.**

a. share
b. toys
c. him
d. Joe

**7. Do you like soccer?**

a. Do
b. like
c. soccer
d. you

**8. Are we almost there yet?**

a. we
b. almost
c. Are
d. there

**9. The teacher will read us a chapter from a book.**

a. teacher
b. us
c. read
d. book

**10. Bears eat a lot before they sleep all winter.**

a. they
b. Bears
c. eat
d. sleep

# Possessive Pronouns

Possessive pronouns are words that show a relationship between a person or a thing, and another person or thing. We call that ownership, or possession.

Of course, if you say *My dad is a police officer*, it doesn't really mean you own your dad, or possess him. That's just what we call these pronouns.

There are lots of possessive pronouns. Words like *my, mine, your, yours, its, our, ours, theirs, his, her* and *hers* are possessive pronouns.

Let's practice with possessive pronouns. Each problem below has a blank where a possessive pronoun should be. Pick the answer that has the possessive pronoun that should go there.

**1. My cousins are late because ____ plane was late.**

a. its
b. ours
c. their
d. mine

**2. Are those ____ shoes?**

a. your
b. yours
c. mine
d. theirs

**3. The team won ____ last 3 games.**

a. theirs
b. ours
c. its
d. mine

**4. Mr. Hernandez said ___ dog had puppies.**

a. mine
b. his
c. hers
d. ours

**5. My sister likes ____ new teacher.**

a. her
b. hers
c. its
d. ours

# Indefinite Pronouns

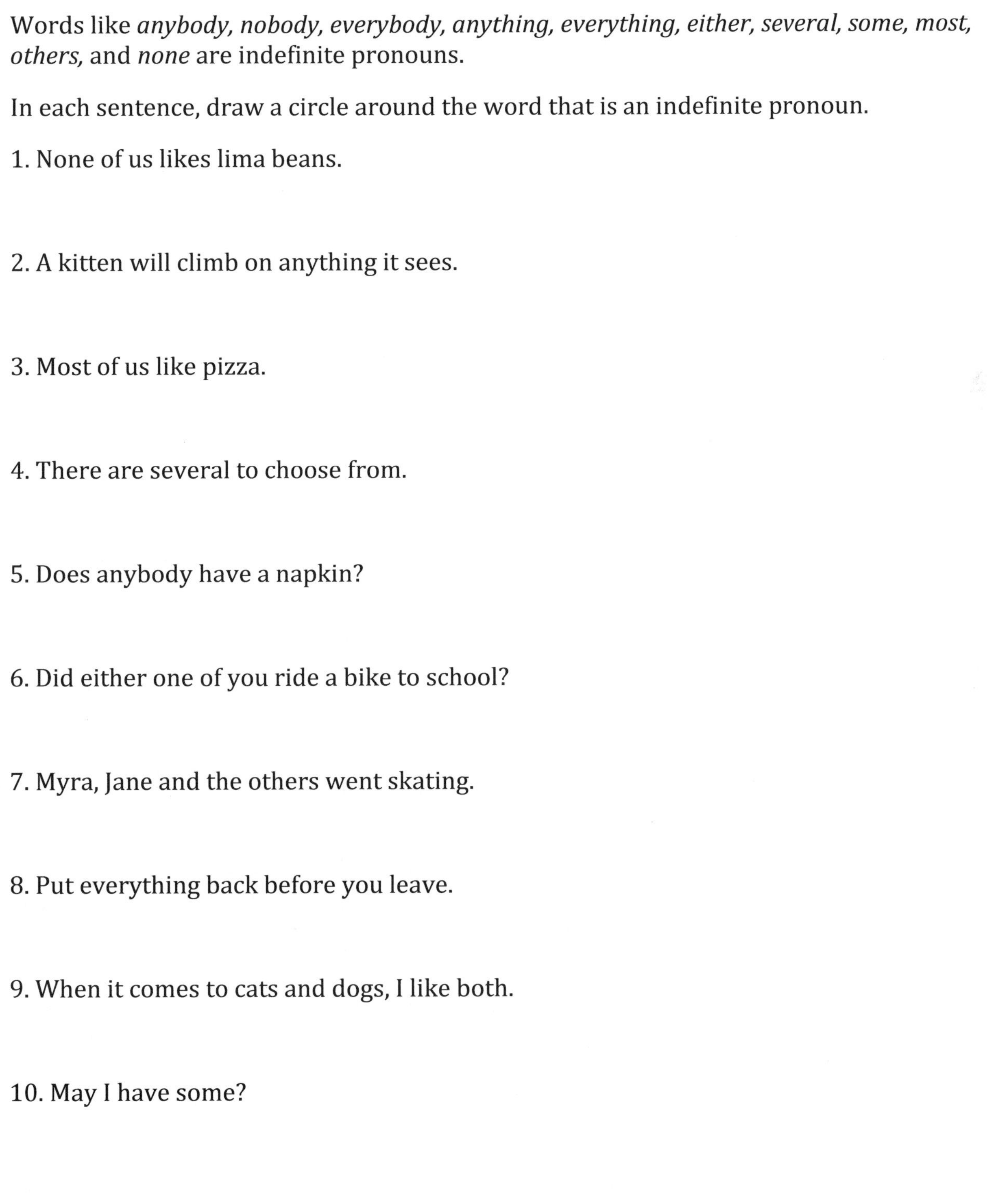

Most pronouns refer to a particular person, place or thing, or particular persons, places or things.

Some pronouns don't refer to particular people or things. These pronouns are called indefinite pronouns.

Words like *anybody, nobody, everybody, anything, everything, either, several, some, most, others,* and *none* are indefinite pronouns.

In each sentence, draw a circle around the word that is an indefinite pronoun.

1. None of us likes lima beans.

2. A kitten will climb on anything it sees.

3. Most of us like pizza.

4. There are several to choose from.

5. Does anybody have a napkin?

6. Did either one of you ride a bike to school?

7. Myra, Jane and the others went skating.

8. Put everything back before you leave.

9. When it comes to cats and dogs, I like both.

10. May I have some?

## Verbs

Verbs are words that show action, or something a person or thing does. Words *like run, walk, jump, take, swing, think, sit, give, pray,* and *talk* are verbs.

Each line has three words. One of the words is a verb. Circle the word that is a verb.

| | | | |
|---|---|---|---|
| 1. | toe | fun | run |
| 2. | bone | skin | walk |
| 3. | teacher | talk | school |
| 4. | kick | sky | red |
| 5. | cat | send | nose |
| 6. | drive | car | silly |
| 7. | brownie | cookie | bake |
| 8. | round | ball | throw |
| 9. | ice | cold | freeze |
| 10. | kitchen | pan | put |

## Subject Verb Agreement

Do you know what a subject is? A subject is a noun or pronoun that a verb refers to. Here are some examples:

*He runs fast.*

In this sentence, the verb is *runs*, and the subject is *he*.

*They run fast.*

In this sentence, the verb is *run*, and the subject is *they*.

Verbs and subjects must agree with each other. That is just a way of saying that you can't use the same kind of verb for every noun or pronoun. This is not always true, but it is true most of the time.

There are singular verbs, and there are plural verbs. Some subjects are one person, place, or thing. These are called singular subjects. You must use a singular verb with them.

Some subjects are more than one person, place, or thing. These are called plural subjects. You must use a plural verb for them.

Let's practice using singular and plural verbs.

**1. Sally __________ her bike to school.**

a. ride
b. rided
c. rides

**2. Sally and Jackie __________ their bikes to school.**

a. ride
b. rided
c. rides

**3. Cindy and James __________ next door.**

a. lives
b. live
c. living

**4. LaShawn __________ next door.**

a. lives
b. live
c. living

**5. Patty __________ six years old.**

a. are
b. be
c. is

**6. The twins __________ six years old.**

a. be
b. are
c. am

**7. Mom and Dad __________ me with homework.**

a. helps
b. help
c. helping

**8. Mom __________ me with my homework.**

a. helping
b. help
c. helps

**9. Pedro __________ tasty cookies.**

a. baking
b. bakes
c. bake

**10. My two sisters __________ tasty cookies.**

a. bake
b. bakes
c. baking

# Verb Tenses

Verbs show action. They can show something that is happening right now. They can also show something that already happened. Or they can show actions that are going to happen later.

We use different forms of a verb to show if an action is happening right now, or if has already happened, or if it will happen later.

These different verb forms are called tenses. Let's practice using them.

For each picture, there will be three sentences. Match the sentence to the correct verb tense: PAST, PRESENT, or FUTURE. If the verb shows something that already happened, draw a line from the sentence to PAST. If the verb shows something happening right now, draw a line from the sentence to PRESENT. If the verb shows something that will happen later, draw a line from the sentence to FUTURE.

1. a. Jack will fly a kite. PAST

   b. Jack flies a kite. PRESENT

   c. Jack flew a kite. FUTURE

2. a. Becky rides her bike. PAST

   b. Becky will ride her bike. PRESENT

   c. Becky rode her bike. FUTURE

3. a. Fluffy ate her food. PAST

b. Fluffy will eat her food. PRESENT

c. Fluffy eats her food FUTURE

4. a. The bird will fly. PAST

b. The bird flies. PRESENT

c. The bird flew. FUTURE

5. a. The fish swam. PAST

b. The fish will swim. PRESENT

c. The fish swims. FUTURE

## Adjectives

Adjectives are words that go with nouns. They tell us what kind of a person, place, or thing we're talking about. Here are some examples:

*The pony is fast.*

What kind of pony is it? It is a *fast* pony. *Fast* is the adjective that tells us what kind of pony it is.

*Wanda has long hair.*

What kind of hair does Wanda have? She has *long* hair. *Long* tells us what kind of hair Wanda has.

Can you think of some more adjectives? Sure you can. You use adjectives all the time.

Here are some that you use all the time: *big, little, red, blue, yellow, slow, short, funny, friendly, hard, soft, furry, nice, bad, good, mad, silly, pretty, easy*. There are lots and lots more, too. Adjectives are everywhere when you look for them.

Sometimes a noun can have more than one adjective. Look at this sentence:

*I have a new blue suit.*

In that sentence, *new* and *blue* are both adjectives that tell us what kind of suit it is.

Let's practice with adjectives. Read these sentences. Then answer the questions after each sentence.

**1. The new puppy is sleeping.**

a. ____________ is the adjective.
b. ____________ is the noun.

**2. The baby is chubby.**

a. ____________ is the adjective.
b. ____________ is the noun.

**3. Recess is fun.**

a. ____________ is the adjective.
b. ____________ is the noun.

**4. The loud alarm woke me up.**

a. ____________ is the adjective.
b. ____________ is the noun.

**5. Amber was happy.**

a. ____________ is the adjective.
b. ____________ is the noun.

# Conjunctions

Conjunctions are words that join two words, or two parts of a sentence. You use conjunctions every day. Here are some you use: *so, yet, or, but, nor, and, for.* Here are some examples:

*Micah and Jonah are coming over.*

In that sentence, *and* joins Micah and Jonah together.

*Do you want milk or water?*

In that sentence, *or* joins milk and water together.

Now it's your turn. In these sentences, draw a circle around the conjunction.

**1. It's time for bed.**

**2. We can eat lunch, or we can wait.**

**3. Tom is coming, but Amy isn't.**

**4. Please move so I can see the TV.**

**5. We sang, and our parents listened.**

# Determiners

A determiner is a word we use with a noun. It comes before the noun and tells the reader whether or not a specific noun is being referred to. Here are some examples:

*I ate the cookie.*

In this sentence, the determiner is *the*.

*I like these toys.*

In this sentence, *these* is the determiner.

Here are some sentences. In each sentence, draw a circle around the determiner.

**1. I have a cold.**

**2. Do you like this dress?**

**3. No; I like that dress.**

**4. These shoes are brown.**

**5. Are those shoes new?**

# Prepositions

Prepositions are special words. They go with nouns or pronouns. They are about when or where, or about ownership. You use prepositions all the time. Here are some examples:

*Put the ball down.*

In this sentence, *down* is the preposition. It is about where.

*Let's wait until Dad gets home.*

In this sentence, *until* is the preposition. It is about when.

*Mr. Grumples is the name of the puppy.*

In this sentence, *of* is the preposition. It shows ownership.

There are over 100 prepositions. Some of the most common are *about, around, below, behind, down, from, in, inside, into, near, off, on, over, through, to, toward, under,* and *with*.

Let's practice. In each sentence, there is a blank. For each sentence, choose the answer that should fill in the blank.

**1. Mrs. Gonzales is the name ____ my teacher.**

a. in
b. Mr.
c. up
d. of

**2. This ball belongs ____ Ramona.**

a. from
b. of
c. to
d. new

**3. I like jelly ____ my toast.**

a. up
b. on
c. in
d. of

**4. Let's run ____ the park.**

a. of
b. with
c. up
d. to

**5. Juan is ____ Dallas, Texas.**

a. to
b. at
c. down
d. from

# Capitalization

## Rule 1: First Word in a Sentence

The first word of every sentence should always be capitalized.

Practice this with these sentences. Underline the word that should be capitalized.

**1. a bear can sleep all winter.**

**2. boys and girls both like playing at recess.**

**3. chess is a fun game that makes you think ahead.**

**4. don't forget your umbrella!**

**5. eating too much candy can make you sick.**

**6. frogs like to eat flies and other bugs.**

**7. going to Sea World last year was my best trip ever.**

**8. how long does it take for cookies to bake?**

**9. it rained all day yesterday.**

**10. joining Boy Scouts is one of the best things I ever did.**

**11. keeping up with homework is easy if you do it before you go out and play.**

**12. let's go see what Mom is making for supper.**

**13. my uncle is a park ranger and works every day in the forest.**

**14. now I'm going to do a magic trick.**

**15. painting can be fun, but it can be messy, too.**

**16. reading books is one of the best ways to spend your spare time.**

**17. quiet, please; it's time to begin.**

**18. six plus two equals eight.**

**19. taking a bath every night keeps us clean.**

**20. you should always look both ways before crossing a street.**

## Rule 2: Pronoun "I"

The pronoun *I* should always be capitalized in a sentence, every time it appears.

Practice this with these sentences. Underline the word that should be capitalized.

**1. When it rains i will get wet if i forget my umbrella.**

**2. i really enjoy playing baseball.**

**3 My cat purrs when i pet her.**

**4. My dog will sit up and beg when i give him a treat.**

**5. When school is called off after it snows, i enjoy sleeping late.**

**6. Today i found a quarter on the sidewalk.**

**7. If my parents say it's OK, i want you to come over this Saturday.**

**8. Going to the dentist is something i don't enjoy.**

**9. If you will help me with my homework, i will help you do the dishes.**

**10. i helped mom make breakfast in bed for Dad on Father's Day.**

**11. We found a stray kitten yesterday, and i helped feed it with a bottle.**

**12. On September 27th, i will turn seven years old.**

**13. When school is out for the summer, i will be going to North Dakota to visit my grandparents.**

**14. Every night before i go to sleep, my parents pray with me and then tuck me in.**

**15. When i grow up i want to be a firefighter.**

**16. My piggy bank is getting full, so i will empty it soon and count my money.**

**17. Last week i scored a run for my Little League team.**

**18. On Fridays i like to ride my bike to school.**

**19. If Dad takes the new job, i will be moving to Indiana.**

**20. Mom told me i need a haircut.**

## Rule 3: Proper Nouns

All names should be capitalized. These are called proper nouns. They include the names of people, groups, teams, companies, and pets, and many more. This also includes nicknames, and titles.

Practice this with these sentences. Underline the words that should be capitalized.

**1. dad and I went to a new grocery store called hanover's.**

**2. I asked mrs. benson if I could have more mashed potatoes.**

**3. Our parents got us two kittens, and lateesha and I named them fluffy and tiger.**

**4. My favorite football team is the dallas cowboys.**

**5. Last week doctor smith said I will need braces.**

**6. Our new priest is father rodriguez.**

**7. We're having a birthday party for uncle bob tonight.**

**8. On Sunday we have lunch with grandma and grandpa after church.**

**9. Did mom talk to your parents about the slumber party?**

**10. I have a sister named joan, but we all call her cissy.**

## Rule 4: Places

The names of cities, towns, states, countries, and continents should always be capitalized. The specific name of any place, such as a park, or a neighborhood, or even a planet or star, should also be capitalized.

Practice this with these sentences. Underline the word that should be capitalized.

**1. My friend Pierre moved here from canada.**

**2. Tommy plays soccer at rogers park on the weekends.**

**3. There are over a hundred nations in africa.**

**4. Last year we visited the empire state building.**

**5. The Chicago Cubs play their home games at wrigley field.**

**6. My cousin lives in fargo, north Dakota.**

**7. My mom and dad are going to take our family on a trip to paris, france, next year.**

**8. I want to be the first human to walk on mars.**

**9. My aunt and uncle live in a huge house in atlanta.**

**10. The city of chicago, illinois, is located in cook county.**

## Rule 5: Dates

All days of the week should start with a capital letter. These are Monday, Tuesday, Wednesday, Thursday, Friday, Saturday, and Sunday.

All months should start with a capital letter. These are January, February, March, April, May, June, July, August, September, October, November, and December.

Let's practice. Write your answers to these questions. If you need help, ask your Mom or Dad, or another adult.

**1. What date is Christmas?**

______________________________

**2. What date is the first day of the year?**

______________________________

**3. What is the first day of the school week?**

______________________________

**4. The day between Thursday and Saturday is what day?**

______________________________

**5. What month does Thanksgiving fall in?**

______________________________

## More Capitalization Questions

Remember these rules – all these words should be capitalized: The first word in a sentence, the word *I*, the names of people and animals, the names of groups or teams, days of the week, months, holidays, cities, towns, states, countries, continents, and other places, the names of companies or businesses, job titles that are used as a form of address, such as Officer Brown and Reverend Archer, relationship based titles used as a form of address (Aunt Rochelle, Uncle Henry), book titles and movie titles, etc.

In the questions below, some words in the sentence should be capitalized, but aren't. Underline the words that should be capitalized, but aren't.

**1. today is monday.**

**2. i will be seven years old on june 1st.**

**3. My friend sally is wearing a blue dress.**

**4. Don't miss out on the christmas light show.**

**5. I went with my dad to burger town for lunch on saturday.**

**6. My cat's name is bonnie.**

**7. For thanksgiving we are going to dallas to visit my grandparents.**

**8. How are you today, grandma?**

**9. Mr. smith is wearing a blue suit.**

**10. Is it time for lunch yet, billy?**

**11. In church, reverend biggs told us a bible story.**

12. Principal jones is also the baseball coach.

13. Coach jones is also the school principal.

14. Aunt sally is coming over for sunday dinner.

15. On sunday my aunt is coming over for dinner.

16. My mom went to a college in ohio.

17. Dad went to wabash college in indiana.

18. The capital of kentucky is frankfort.

19. there are six flags in the parking lot.

20. I like going to six flags, the amusement park.

21. Our teacher is reading a book called my friend flicka to us.

22. At first, there were only 13 states in the united states of america.

23. we go to church almost every sunday.

24. We attend morning valley baptist church.

25. I gave dad a present for father's day.

## Punctuation

A sentence that makes a statement should end with a period (.).

A sentence that asks a question should end with a question mark (?).

A sentence that expresses powerful feelings should end with an exclamation point (!).

Read the following sentences and choose the correct end punctuation for each one.

**1. Becky enjoys playing with dolls**

a. period
b. question mark
c. exclamation point

**2. Are you going to the ball game**

a. period
b. question mark
c. exclamation point

**3. My dog likes to play fetch**

a. period
b. question mark
c. exclamation point

**4. You are the best dog in the whole wide world**

a. period
b. question mark
c. exclamation point

**5. When did Mom say we're going to the store**

a. period
b. question mark
c. exclamation point

**6. What a scary story**

a. period
b. question mark
c. exclamation point

**7. This is so exciting**

a. period
b. question mark
c. exclamation point

**8. My dad asked me if I like math**

a. period
b. question mark
c. exclamation point

**9. I like going to the county fair and eating corn dogs**

a. period
b. question mark
c. exclamation point

**10. Is it almost time for supper**

a. period
b. question mark
c. exclamation point

# Commas

## Rule 1: Use Commas With A List

Commas are used in between some words. They can be used to separate a long list of words. Here are some examples:

*Jimmy, Billy, Sally, Frank, Pedro, and Tommy are in the band.*

*We had pizza, hot dogs, punch, and cookies.*

Don't forget to put the word *and* after the last comma in a list.

Let's practice. Rewrite these sentences using commas in the right spots.

**1. I ride to school with Cindy Bob LaShawn and Manny.**

______________________________

______________________________

**2. The names of the flowers are tulips roses daffodils and lilies.**

______________________________

______________________________

**3. Joe Mark and Greg are the tallest boys in the class.**

______________________________

______________________________

**4. I like football baseball soccer and basketball.**

______________________________

______________________________

**5. Red blue and yellow are her favorite colors.**

______________________________

______________________________

## Rule 2: Use Commas Between Cities And States

A comma should always separate a city and a state.

*Dayton, Ohio*

*Hammond, Indiana*

*Fort Worth, Texas*

Here are some you can try. Rewrite these with a comma in the right spot.

**1. Houston Texas**

**2. Akron Ohio**

**3. New York New York**

**4. Nashville Tennessee**

**5. Salt Lake City Utah**

## RULE 3: USE COMMAS IN DATES

A comma should be used to separate the date and year when writing a date:

*July 4, 1776*

*April 22, 2012*

*December 7, 1941*

Now here are five you can try. Rewrite these dates with the comma in the right spot.

**1. March 15 1985**

**2. June 2 2022**

**3. July 10 1959**

**4. October 30 1492**

**5. August 15 1979**

# Letter Practice

Look at the picture. Then print the first letter of the object in upper case (big), and then in lower case (little).

1.  __________ and __________

2.  __________ and __________ 

3.  __________ and __________

4. __________ and __________ 

5.  __________ and __________

6. ____________ and ____________ 

7.  ____________ and ____________

8. ____________ and ____________ 

9.  ____________ and ____________

10. ____________ and ____________ 

11.  ____________ and ____________

12. ____________ and ____________

13. ____________ and ____________

14. ____________ and ____________

15. ____________ and ____________

16. ____________ and ____________

17.  ____________ and ____________

18. ____________ and ____________

19.

____________ and ____________

20. ____________ and ____________

21.

____________ and ____________

22. ____________ and ____________

23.

____________ and ____________

24. ____________ and ____________

25.  ____________ and ____________

26. ____________ and ____________

## Same Word, Different Meanings

Some words have more than one meaning. Look at each problem below. Each problem has two sentences, with a blank space. For each problem, fill in the blanks with the word that makes sense. Remember, both sentences must have the same word.

1.

I like to _____________ sports on TV with my dad.

I know what time it is by looking at my _____________.

---

2.

We will _____________ the car here and walk to the store.

We had fun playing soccer at the _____________.

---

3.

This bag of groceries isn't heavy; it's _____________.

I turned on the _____________.

---

4.

I am learning how to ____________ my name in cursive.

You must always stop at a stop ____________.

5.

It cools off and leaves turn brown in the ____________.

If you don't wear a belt your pants will ____________ down.

6.

Twelve inches equals one ____________.

A ____________ has five toes.

7.

I have a dollar and some ____________ in my pocket.

The light bulb is burned out, so I will ____________ it.

8.

A stick will float on water, but a rock will
_____________.

Put the dirty dishes in the ______.

9.

I taught my dog to _____________over for a treat.

I put butter on my _____________ at dinner.

10.

Our class went on a field _____________ to a dairy farm.

Pick up your toys, or someone may _____________ over them.

## Prefixes and Suffixes

Prefixes and suffixes are important parts of some words. Prefixes are part of the word at the beginning, and suffixes are part of the word at the end. Both prefixes and suffixes change the meaning of the word.

Answer the following questions about words that have prefixes and suffixes.

**1. What do we call a person who writes for a living?**

a. writing
b. rewrite
c. writed
d. writer

**2. What kind of classes do kids go to when they're 3 or 4 years old?**

a. afterschool
b. preschool
c. earlyschool
d. firstschool

**3. To take off our seat belt, what do we do?**

a. rebuckle it
b. unbuckle it
c. postbuckle it
d. prebuckle it

**4. If I am more happy today than yesterday, what am I?**

a. happier
b. happiest
c. happymost
d. nonhappy

**5. What is another way of saying we go to church every week?**

a. we go to church preweek
b. we go to church postweek
c. we go to church weekest
d. we go to church weekly

# Writing

## My Favorite ____________________

Write about something you like a lot. It could be a toy, or a sport, or a team, or a game, or a pet, or a book, or a movie, or anything else. Tell a little bit about it, so people get a good idea of what you're writing about. Then say why you like it so much. You can give more than one reason. And then write an ending to wrap it up.

## All About ____________

Choose something you know about, and write about it. Your report should help the reader understand more about the topic. Give some facts about your topic to help readers understand. The last part should let the reader know that it's the end of your report.

## My School Day

Write about two or three things that happened to you at school recently. Make sure you tell them in order, and give details so readers can understand. The last part should be a good ending.

# Practice Test #1

*Questions 1-3 are about the following story:*

**My Trip to the Beach**

Last weekend my family took a trip to the beach. We got there before noon. The sun was very high in the sky, and it was hot! My sister Julie and I could not wait to swim.

We ran right into the ocean, but it was so cold! We only swam for a few minutes before we could not stand the cold anymore. So we ran back out onto the sand. The sun dried us off very quickly. Then we were very hot again! So we ran back into the water. It was still very cold.

Julie said, "Bill, let's get out again."

I said, "Julie, be patient. We might get used to the cold."

And you know what? That is exactly what happened! We swam for a long time. It was a lot of fun!

**1. Who is telling this story?**

a. Bill
b. Julie
c. Bill's mother
d. Julie's father

**2. When does the family get to the beach?**

a. At sunset
b. At noon
c. After noon
d. Before noon

**3. What is the lesson of this story?**

a. Swimming is hard work.
b. It is good to be patient.
c. The beach is fun.
d. Families are always happy.

*Questions 4 and 5 are about the following story:*

**The Play**

Karen and Rudy were bored on Saturday. They did not know what to do.

"I have an idea!" Karen said. "We should put on a play!"

"That's a great idea!" Rudy said.

Rudy and Karen asked all their friends to act in the play.

"I'll be a bear," Sheila said.

"I'll be a deer," Myron said.

"We'll be campers," Karen and Rudy said.

The kids spent all morning making their costumes. Then they invited their parents to the play. The adults sat in Karen's backyard and watched the show. It was about two campers who see a deer in the forest. Then they get chased away by a big bear! All the parents loved the play.

**4. What is true about Karen?**

a. She has good ideas.
b. She likes bears.
c. She goes camping a lot.
d. She does not have a backyard.

**5. If this story were turned into a book, it would be ____________________.**

a. funnier
b. more serious
c. longer
d. less interesting

*Questions 6-8 are about the following story:*

**Cats**

Cats make wonderful pets. Like dogs, they can be very loving. They like to rub up against people with their soft fur. When people pet cats, they purr to show they are happy.

Cats are also good at telling you what they need. They will meow when they are hungry. They will scratch at a door if they want to be let inside.

Sometimes cats like to be left alone, so they will not take up a lot of your time. They sleep more than most other animals. Some cats sleep 16 hours a day! When they wake up, they may want you to play with them. Some cats are shy and would rather hide behind a chair or a desk. But you will see them soon enough when it is feeding time!

**6. Read this sentence from the story:**

Cats make wonderful pets.

**What does wonderful mean?**

a. Very bad
b. Very good
c. Very fast
d. Very sad

**7. What is true about cats?**

a. They all sleep 16 hours a day.
b. They are totally silent.
c. They like to be alone sometimes.
d. They do not like people.

**8. How are cats and dogs alike?**

a. They both purr.
b. They both sleep most of the day.
c. They both meow.
d. They both can be loving.

*Questions 9 and 10 are about the following story:*

**Singing Strings**

No matter what kind of music you like, you have heard the guitar. It is one of the best-loved instruments.

The guitar is a string instrument. Most guitars have six strings. Some have twelve. You can strum the strings all at once. You can also pluck them one at a time. The way you play the strings changes the way the guitar sounds.

The strings stretch over a long piece of wood. This is called the neck. A round hole in the middle of the guitar makes it sound louder. Some guitars do not need this hole. They are electric guitars. They plug into speakers. Speakers make electric guitars louder.

Quiet or loud. Twelve strings or six. Listen to those strings sing! It's the fantastic guitar.

**9. What is this story about?**

a. Singers
b. Speaking
c. The guitar
d. Shoe strings

**10. Read these sentences from a book about guitars:**

A guitar has six strings. Plucking the strings makes sound. The violin also has strings. But these strings are played with a bow.

**What do these sentences tell you that "Singing Strings" does not?**

a. Violins have strings.
b. Guitars have strings.
c. Guitar strings can be plucked.
d. A guitar is played with a bow.

**11. Read this sentence:**

The apple fell from the tree.

**Why does the start with an upper case T in the sentence above?**

a. It is the name of a person.
b. It is the first word of the sentence.
c. It is the name of a place.
d. It is a title.

**12. The e in the word <u>me</u> sounds like the <u>e</u> in ________________.**

a. the
b. pet
c. men
d. see

**13. Which word starts with the same first sound as <u>from</u>?**

a. run
b. food
c. frog
d. for

**14. Which word is spelled right?**

a. blue
b. bloo
c. blu
d. blou

**15. Read this sentence:**

The <u>tiny</u> bug sat on my finger.

**The word <u>tiny</u> means ______________.**

a. very big
b. very small
c. very nice
d. very old

**16. Which word is spelled right?**

a. again
b. agin
c. agan
d. agen

**17. Which word is spelled right?**

a. sinne
b. syn
c. sien
d. sign

**18. Which word is spelled right?**

a. bayby
b. baby
c. baaby
d. baeby

**19. If you love baseball, what is a good title for a story about how much you like it?**

a. "Baseball Is the Best!"
b. "How to Play Baseball"
c. "The History of Baseball"
d. "Bats and Balls"

**20. Which sentence is right?**

a. As I sat in class, I went to school.
b. I was hungry because I ate a sandwich.
c. I went to the zoo and then I saw a lion!
d. I had a dream before I fell asleep.

**21. What could you use to write a story?**

a. A hammer
b. A paintbrush
c. A wrench
d. A computer

**22. What kind of true story could you write without having to read about it first?**

a. A story about how bread is made
b. A story about what you did yesterday
c. A story about why the sun sets
d. A story about different kinds of dogs

**23. What should you do in class?**

a. Talk without raising your hand first
b. Talk while someone else is talking
c. Talk so quiet no one can hear you
d. Talk after your teacher asks you to

**24. What should you do if you do not understand something your teacher said?**

a. Ask your teacher to explain it again
b. Sit quietly and hope you will understand it later
c. Ask your friend what the teacher said
d. Pretend you understand what your teacher said

**25. Which is the best sentence?**

a. My grandfather is a grandfather.
b. My grandfather is a very nice man.
c. My grandfather likes stuff.
d. My grandfather is so.

**26. Which is the best picture to put in a story about fish?**

a.

b.

c.

d.

**27. Which sentence is right?**

a. I went with tommy to the movies.
b. I went with Tommy to the movies.
c. i went with tommy to the movies.
d. i went with Tommy to the Movies.

**28. Which sentence is right?**

a. The girl run on the field.
b. The girls runs on the field.
c. The girl run on the fields.
d. The girl runs on the field.

**29. Which sentence is right?**

a. Tim read a book yesterday.
b. Tim read a book tomorrow.
c. Tim read a book next week.
d. Tim read a book next month.

**30. Which sentence is right?**

a. The cat and the dog played in the yard.
b. The cat for the dog played in the yard.
c. The cat but the dog played in the yard.
d. The cat because the dog played in the yard.

**31. Which sentence is right?**

a. The bird flew under us.
b. The bird flew beneath us.
c. The bird flew through us.
d. The bird flew over us.

**32. Which sentence is right?**

a. My brother's Birthday is may 14th.
b. My brother's birthday is May 14th.
c. My Brother's birthday is may 14th.
d. my brother's birthday is may 14th.

**33. Which sentence is right?**

a. Tina ate cereal fruit and toast for breakfast.
b. Tina ate cereal, fruit, and toast for breakfast.
c. Tina ate cereal fruit, and toast for breakfast.
d. Tina ate cereal fruit and toast, for breakfast.

**34. Look at the picture and say what it is out loud.**

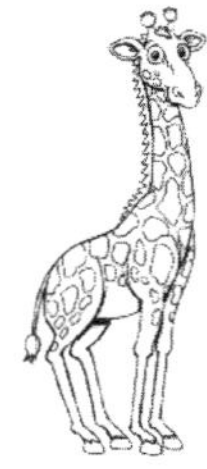

**How do you spell this?**

a. giraffe
b. jurif
c. joraif
d. girolf

**35. The word <u>unhappy</u> means**

a. very happy
b. a little happy
c. not happy
d. pretty happy

**36. Read this list:**

Blue, green, orange, red

**Which other word belongs in this list?**

a. pickle
b. tiger
c. moon
d. yellow

**37. A boat is used for**

a. sailing
b. flying
c. stirring
d. walking

**38. Read this sentence:**

May I ______ say something?

**Which word belongs on the line?**

a. never
b. please
c. time
d. answer

# Practice Test #2

*Numbers 1-3 are about the following story:*

**One Snowy Day**

"Jill! Jill! Wake up!"

It was early Saturday morning. I was very sleepy, but I could hear how excited Mom was. I rubbed my eyes and threw aside the blanket.

"What is it, Mom?" I asked.

"Look out the window, Jill!" Mom said.

I looked out the window. The street was all white! There must have been a snowstorm last night!

"Let's go sledding!" Mom said.

"That sounds great, Mom!" I answered.

Mom and I put our sleds into her car. Then we drove to the park. There were many nice hills there, all smooth with fresh snow.

"Ready?" Mom asked. "Let's go!"

<u>Whoosh</u>! We sped down the hill on our sleds. I love snowy days!

**1. The word Whoosh is used to make you feel the ____________________.**

a. speed of the sleds.
b. color of the snow.
c. warmth of the morning.
d. size of the hills.

**2. What is the park like?**

a. Foggy
b. Wet
c. Tired
d. Snowy

**3. How are Jill and her mom the same?**

a. They both are sleepy.
b. They both like sledding.
c. They both are little girls.
d. They both drive cars.

*Questions 4 and 5 are about the following story:*

**The Farm**

One day, Sammy went to visit his grandparents on their farm. Sammy always loved that old farm. His grandparents had a list of fun things they would do together.

First Sammy and his grandpa went to the chicken coop. Grandpa had a big bag of grain. He scooped some out with a little shovel.

"Open your hands, Sammy," Grandpa said.

Sammy opened his hands. Grandpa poured some grain into them.

"Toss that around the coop, Sammy," Grandpa said.

Sammy tossed the grain. The chickens all came out to eat the grain.

"Boy, Grandpa," Sammy said. "The chickens love that grain!"

Next Sammy joined his grandma in the field. She was digging in the dirt. There was a bag of seed next to her.

"Take some of that seed, Sammy," Grandma said. "Then drop it in this hole I made in the dirt."

Sammy did what his grandma asked him to do.

"That seed will grow into corn," Grandma said.

"Wow!" Sammy said. "I helped feed the chickens so you will have eggs. Then I planted seed so you will have corn. I love working on your farm!"

**4. What does Sammy do first on the farm?**

a. He goes to the field.
b. He plants the corn.
c. He feeds the chickens.
d. He digs a hole.

**5. What is something Sammy sees in the field?**

a. Dirt
b. Corn
c. Hills
d. Paths

*Questions 6-8 are about the following story:*

**Making Art**

Making art can be a lot of fun. One way to make art is painting. You need only a few things to start making a pretty picture.

First you need some paints. A few colors are all you need to start your art. Then you need something to paint on. Use some thick paper if you have it. You can also paint on scraps of cardboard. You will also need a brush. Dip the brush in the paint. Spread the paint on your paper.

What would you like to paint? You can paint anything you can imagine! Make a painting of a horse or a tree. Paint a picture of a dragon or a mermaid. Anything is possible in a painting!

When you are done painting, let your picture dry. The paint may be wet. Then ask an adult to hang your painting on the wall. Go ahead. You did something that should make you feel proud. You just made art!

**6. Which sentence shows that you can paint anything you can imagine?**

a. Making art can be a lot of fun.
b. You will also need a brush.
c. Paint a picture of a dragon or a mermaid.
d. The paint may be wet.

**7. What is this story about?**

a. Where to find cardboard
b. When to start a painting
c. Why artists are smart
d. How to paint a picture

**8. Why does the writer say you should feel proud?**

a. Because you know what a brush is
b. Because you made art
c. Because you have friends
d. Because you let your picture dry

*Questions 9 and 10 are about the following table of contents from a book about monkeys:*

**Monkey Life**

Table of Contents



**9. If you want to know what monkeys eat, you should read**

a. Chapter 1
b. Chapter 2
c. Chapter 3
d. Chapter 4

**10. What does the picture tell you that the table of contents does not?**

a. Monkeys have tails.
b. Monkeys have babies.
c. Monkeys play.
d. Monkeys live in trees.

**11. The o in the word owl sounds like the o in ____________.**

a. tool
b. moon
c. cow
d. toe

**12. Which shows how to sound out the word lamb?**

a. lay-b
b. bl-am
c. lu-mbb
d. la-mm

**13. What is the long vowel sound in the word goat?**

a. oa
b. go
c. at
d. gt

**14. What is a knife?**

a. A bike for riding
b. A color for painting
c. A tool for cutting
d. A tune for singing

**15. Read this sentence:**

All of the sudden, the lion roared!

**How should you read this sentence if you were telling a story?**

a. Quietly
b. Slowly
c. Sleepily
d. Loudly

**16. Which sentence is right?**

a. Who are you.
b. Who are you?
c. Who are you!
d. Who are you

**17. Which word is spelled right?**

a. ear
b. eer
c. eere
d. eaer

**18. Read this sentence:**

The dog likes to gnaw on the bone.

**The word gnaw means**

a. run
b. chew
c. sleep
d. work

**19. What is the best title for a story telling how to play the piano?**

a. "Who Made the Piano?"
b. "Famous Piano Players"
c. "My Favorite Songs"
d. "Playing the Piano"

**20. Before writing a story about birds, you should ________________.**

a. draw a picture of birds
b. sing a song about birds
c. read a book about birds
d. write a poem about birds

**21. Which sentence is right?**

a. The stars shine then the sun sets.
b. I played all day then I took a bath.
c. I fell asleep then Dad told me a story.
d. When the room was bright I turned on the lamp.

**22. What kind of true story could you write without having to read about it first?**

a. A story about the first Thanksgiving
b. A story about leopards
c. A story about your favorite movie
d. A story about who made the first airplane

**23. If your teacher asks you a question about a book you read, you should ________________.**

a. talk about your lunch
b. ask the teacher a question
c. tell the teacher you like football
d. talk about the book

**24. What is the best thing to say after a friend says, "I like reading books"?**

a. I have a pet dog.
b. My favorite color is blue.
c. What is your favorite book?
d. I like watching movies.

**25. What should you say to your teacher if you do not understand a lesson?**

a. Can you explain that again please?
b. Can I be excused?
c. Can we talk about something else?
d. Can I tell the class a story?

**26. Which is the best sentence?**

a. This is book.
b. Show me how to.
c. Book showed cook.
d. This book showed me how to cook.

**27. Which sentence is right?**

a. That is Brians toy.
b. That is Brian's toy.
c. That is Brian toy.
d. That is Brian toy's.

**28. Which sentence is right?**

a. Gail is my best friend.
b. Gail is mine best friend.
c. Gail is me best friend.
d. Gail is I best friend.

**29. Read this sentence:**

The raccoon has a _______ tail.

**Which word best completes this sentence?**

a. slow
b. bad
c. furry
d. loud

**30. Read this sentence:**

Elise ate ____ apple.

**Which word best completes this sentence?**

a. an
b. a
c. these
d. those

**31. Which sentence is the right way to tell someone to do something?**

a. You should come with me?
b. You with me.
c. You with me?
d. You should come with me.

**32. Which sentence is right?**

a. This is the best day of my life
b. This is the best day of my life!
c. This is the best day of my life?
d. This is the best day of my life,

**33. Which word is spelled right?**

a. ekko
b. eccco
c. echo
d. ehco

**34. Read this sentence:**

When Fred goes to the beach, Petra will <u>remain</u> at home.

**What does the word <u>remain</u> mean?**

a. Go
b. Swim
c. Jog
d. Stay

**35. Read this sentence:**

I am _____ about my day.

**Which word best completes this sentence?**

a. think
b. thinking
c. thinks
d. thought

**36. Read this sentence:**

The swan flew into the lake and floated.

**A swan is a ___________________.**

a. bird that swims
b. kind of fish
c. plant that flies
d. funny animal

**37. Read the sentence:**

The mountain is ________.

**Which word best completes this sentence?**

a. small
b. skinny
c. huge
d. big

**38. Read this list.**

one
three
four
six

**Which word belongs in this list?**

a. you
b. two
c. soft
d. hand

# Success Strategies

The most important thing you can do is to ignore your fears and jump into the test immediately- do not be overwhelmed by any strange-sounding terms. You have to jump into the test like jumping into a pool- all at once is the easiest way.

## Make Predictions

As you read and understand the question, try to guess what the answer will be. Remember that several of the answer choices are wrong, and once you begin reading them, your mind will immediately become cluttered with answer choices designed to throw you off. Your mind is typically the most focused immediately after you have read the question and digested its contents. If you can, try to predict what the correct answer will be. You may be surprised at what you can predict.

Quickly scan the choices and see if your prediction is in the listed answer choices. If it is, then you can be quite confident that you have the right answer. It still won't hurt to check the other answer choices, but most of the time, you've got it!

## Answer the Question

It may seem obvious to only pick answer choices that answer the question, but the test writers can create some excellent answer choices that are wrong. Don't pick an answer just because it sounds right, or you believe it to be true. It MUST answer the question. Once you've made your selection, always go back and check it against the question and make sure that you didn't misread the question, and the answer choice does answer the question posed.

## Benchmark

After you read the first answer choice, decide if you think it sounds correct or not. If it doesn't, move on to the next answer choice. If it does, mentally mark that answer choice. This doesn't mean that you've definitely selected it as your answer choice, it just means that it's the best you've seen thus far. Go ahead and read the next choice. If the next choice is worse than the one you've already selected, keep going to the next answer choice. If the next choice is better than the choice you've already selected, mentally mark the new answer choice as your best guess.

The first answer choice that you select becomes your standard. Every other answer choice must be benchmarked against that standard. That choice is correct until proven otherwise by another answer choice beating it out. Once you've decided that no other answer choice seems as good, do one final check to ensure that your answer choice answers the question posed.

## Valid Information

Don't discount any of the information provided in the question. Every piece of information may be necessary to determine the correct answer. None of the information in the question is there to throw you off (while the answer choices will certainly have information to throw you off). If two seemingly unrelated topics are discussed, don't ignore either. You can be confident there is a relationship, or it wouldn't be included in the question, and you are probably going to have to determine what is that relationship to find the answer.

### Avoid "Fact Traps"

Don't get distracted by a choice that is factually true. Your search is for the answer that answers the question. Stay focused and don't fall for an answer that is true but incorrect. Always go back to the question and make sure you're choosing an answer that actually answers the question and is not just a true statement. An answer can be factually correct, but it MUST answer the question asked. Additionally, two answers can both be seemingly correct, so be sure to read all of the answer choices, and make sure that you get the one that BEST answers the question.

### Milk the Question

Some of the questions may throw you completely off. They might deal with a subject you have not been exposed to, or one that you haven't reviewed in years. While your lack of knowledge about the subject will be a hindrance, the question itself can give you many clues that will help you find the correct answer. Read the question carefully and look for clues. Watch particularly for adjectives and nouns describing difficult terms or words that you don't recognize. Regardless of if you completely understand a word or not, replacing it with a synonym either provided or one you more familiar with may help you to understand what the questions are asking. Rather than wracking your mind about specific detailed information concerning a difficult term or word, try to use mental substitutes that are easier to understand.

### The Trap of Familiarity

Don't just choose a word because you recognize it. On difficult questions, you may not recognize a number of words in the answer choices. The test writers don't put "make-believe" words on the test; so don't think that just because you only recognize all the words in one answer choice means that answer choice must be correct. If you only recognize words in one answer choice, then focus on that one. Is it correct? Try your best to determine if it is correct. If it is, that is great, but if it doesn't, eliminate it. Each word and answer choice you eliminate increases your chances of getting the question correct, even if you then have to guess among the unfamiliar choices.

### Eliminate Answers

Eliminate choices as soon as you realize they are wrong. But be careful! Make sure you consider all of the possible answer choices. Just because one appears right, doesn't mean that the next one won't be even better! The test writers will usually put more than one good answer choice for every question, so read all of them. Don't worry if you are stuck between two that seem right. By getting down to just two remaining possible choices, your odds are now 50/50. Rather than wasting too much time, play the odds. You are guessing, but guessing wisely, because you've been able to knock out some of the answer choices that you know are wrong. If you are eliminating choices and realize that the last answer choice you are left with is also obviously wrong, don't panic. Start over and consider each choice again. There may easily be something you missed the first time and will realize on the second pass.

### Tough Questions

If you are stumped on a problem or it appears too hard or too difficult, don't waste time. Move on! Remember though, if you can quickly check for obviously incorrect answer choices, your chances of guessing correctly are greatly improved. Before you completely give up, at least try to knock out a couple of possible answers. Eliminate what you can and then guess at the remaining answer choices before moving on.

### Brainstorm

If you get stuck on a difficult question, spend a few seconds quickly brainstorming. Run through the complete list of possible answer choices. Look at each choice and ask yourself, "Could this answer the question satisfactorily?" Go through each answer choice and consider it independently of the other. By systematically going through all possibilities, you may find something that you would otherwise overlook. Remember that when you get stuck, it's important to try to keep moving.

### Read Carefully

Understand the problem. Read the question and answer choices carefully. Don't miss the question because you misread the terms. You have plenty of time to read each question thoroughly and make sure you understand what is being asked. Yet a happy medium must be attained, so don't waste too much time. You must read carefully, but efficiently.

### Face Value

When in doubt, use common sense. Always accept the situation in the problem at face value. Don't read too much into it. These problems will not require you to make huge leaps of logic. The test writers aren't trying to throw you off with a cheap trick. If you have to go beyond creativity and make a leap of logic in order to have an answer choice answer the question, then you should look at the other answer choices. Don't overcomplicate the problem by creating theoretical relationships or explanations that will warp time or space. These are normal problems rooted in reality. It's just that the applicable relationship or explanation may not be readily apparent and you have to figure things out. Use your common sense to interpret anything that isn't clear.

### Prefixes

If you're having trouble with a word in the question or answer choices, try dissecting it. Take advantage of every clue that the word might include. Prefixes and suffixes can be a huge help. Usually they allow you to determine a basic meaning. Pre- means before, post- means after, pro - is positive, de- is negative. From these prefixes and suffixes, you can get an idea of the general meaning of the word and try to put it into context. Beware though of any traps. Just because con is the opposite of pro, doesn't necessarily mean congress is the opposite of progress!

### Hedge Phrases

Watch out for critical "hedge" phrases, such as likely, may, can, will often, sometimes, often, almost, mostly, usually, generally, rarely, sometimes. Question writers insert these hedge phrases to cover every possibility. Often an answer choice will be wrong simply because it leaves no room for exception. Avoid answer choices that have definitive words like "exactly," and "always".

## Switchback Words

Stay alert for "switchbacks". These are the words and phrases frequently used to alert you to shifts in thought. The most common switchback word is "but". Others include although, however, nevertheless, on the other hand, even though, while, in spite of, despite, regardless of.

## New Information

Correct answer choices will rarely have completely new information included. Answer choices typically are straightforward reflections of the material asked about and will directly relate to the question. If a new piece of information is included in an answer choice that doesn't even seem to relate to the topic being asked about, then that answer choice is likely incorrect. All of the information needed to answer the question is usually provided for you, and so you should not have to make guesses that are unsupported or choose answer choices that require unknown information that cannot be reasoned on its own.

## Time Management

On technical questions, don't get lost on the technical terms. Don't spend too much time on any one question. If you don't know what a term means, then since you don't have a dictionary, odds are you aren't going to get much further. You should immediately recognize terms as whether or not you know them. If you don't, work with the other clues that you have, the other answer choices and terms provided, but don't waste too much time trying to figure out a difficult term.

## Contextual Clues

Look for contextual clues. An answer can be right but not correct. The contextual clues will help you find the answer that is most right and is correct. Understand the context in which a phrase or statement is made. This will help you make important distinctions.

## Don't Panic

Panicking will not answer any questions for you. Therefore, it isn't helpful. When you first see the question, if your mind goes blank, take a deep breath. Force yourself to mechanically go through the steps of solving the problem and using the strategies you've learned.

## Pace Yourself

Don't get clock fever. It's easy to be overwhelmed when you're looking at a page full of questions, your mind is full of random thoughts and feeling confused, and the clock is ticking down faster than you would like. Calm down and maintain the pace that you have set for yourself. As long as you are on track by monitoring your pace, you are guaranteed to have enough time for yourself. When you get to the last few minutes of the test, it may seem like you won't have enough time left, but if you only have as many questions as you should have left at that point, then you're right on track!

## Answer Selection

The best way to pick an answer choice is to eliminate all of those that are wrong, until only one is left and confirm that is the correct answer. Sometimes though, an answer choice may immediately look right. Be careful! Take a second to make sure that the other choices are not equally obvious. Don't make a hasty mistake. There are only two times that you should stop before checking other answers. First is when you are positive that the answer choice you have selected is correct. Second is when time is almost out and you have to make a quick guess!

## Check Your Work

Since you will probably not know every term listed and the answer to every question, it is important that you get credit for the ones that you do know. Don't miss any questions through careless mistakes. If at all possible, try to take a second to look back over your answer selection and make sure you've selected the correct answer choice and haven't made a costly careless mistake (such as marking an answer choice that you didn't mean to mark). This quick double check should more than pay for itself in caught mistakes for the time it costs.

## Beware of Directly Quoted Answers

Sometimes an answer choice will repeat word for word a portion of the question or reference section. However, beware of such exact duplication – it may be a trap! More than likely, the correct choice will paraphrase or summarize a point, rather than being exactly the same wording.

## Slang

Scientific sounding answers are better than slang ones. An answer choice that begins "To compare the outcomes…" is much more likely to be correct than one that begins "Because some people insisted…"

## Extreme Statements

Avoid wild answers that throw out highly controversial ideas that are proclaimed as established fact. An answer choice that states the "process should be used in certain situations, if…" is much more likely to be correct than one that states the "process should be discontinued completely." The first is a calm rational statement and doesn't even make a definitive, uncompromising stance, using a hedge word "if" to provide wiggle room, whereas the second choice is a radical idea and far more extreme.

## Answer Choice Families

When you have two or more answer choices that are direct opposites or parallels, one of them is usually the correct answer. For instance, if one answer choice states "x increases" and another answer choice states "x decreases" or "y increases," then those two or three answer choices are very similar in construction and fall into the same family of answer choices. A family of answer choices is when two or three answer choices are very similar in construction, and yet often have a directly opposite meaning. Usually the correct answer choice will be in that family of answer choices. The "odd man out" or answer choice that doesn't seem to fit the parallel construction of the other answer choices is more likely to be incorrect.

## Online Resources

Due to our efforts to try to keep this book to a manageable length, we've created a link that will give you access to all of your online resources:

**mometrix.com/resources719/ssterrag1rlwb**

# It's Your Moment, Let's Celebrate It!

**Share your story @mometrixtestpreparation**

# Table of Contents

# Workbook Answers

## Reading: Informational Texts

### All About Corn

**1. C:** Corn is grown on farms.

**2. D:** Corn plants are called stalks.

**3. B:** Stalks of corn are very tall.

**4. C:** The part of the stalk that has the corn is an ear.

### All About Birds

**1. D:** Most birds live in trees.

**2. A:** Birds can fly because they have wings.

**3. B:** Baby birds eat worms and bugs and seeds.

**4. B:** Birds use leaves and twigs to make a nest.

### Ronald Reagan

**1. D:** The passage is mainly about the life of Ronald Reagan.

**2. C:** Ronald Reagan went to college in the same state where he grew up, Illinois.

**3. D:** A person who saves people from drowning is called a lifeguard.

**4. A:** Ronald Reagan saved 77 people from drowning when he was a lifeguard.

**5. A:** Ronald Reagan's first job after college was at a radio station.

**6. C:** Ronald Reagan defeated Jimmy Carter by getting more votes than him and becoming President.

**7. C:** Ronald Reagan was elected Governor of California.

**8. A:** Ronald Reagan was President of the United States from 1981 to 1989.

## Molly's Chores

**1a.** 7

**1b.** Words

**2a.** 2

**2b.** Pictures

**3a.** Sweep

**3b.** Words

**4a.** 3

**4b.** Pictures

**5a.** Yes

**5b.** Pictures

## 50 Different States

**1.** Kansas should connect to the wheat field.

**2.** Florida should connect to the orange tree.

**3.** Arizona should connect to the Grand Canyon.

**4.** Utah should connect to the ski slope.

**5.** Texas should connect to the person running on a hot day.

## The Big Game

**1. D**

**2. B**

**3. A**

**4. B**

**5. B**

## What's Different? What's the Same?

1. A

2. B

3. B

4. C

5. C

6. B

7. B

8. C

# Reading: Literature

## Billy and His Brother

**1. C:** Billy was in the living room.

**2. A:** Billy was sitting on the couch.

**3. C:** Billy's cat was on the chair.

**4. D:** Billy's brother wanted to sit in the chair.

## Cindy in the Kitchen

**1. C:** Helping her mom in the kitchen made Cindy feel like a big girl.

**2. B:** Cindy almost put too much milk in the cookie dough.

**3. C:** This was the first time Cindy got to help her mom make cookies.

**4. A:** Cindy's mom put the extra cookies in a cookie jar.

**5. D:** The main idea of the story is about Cindy helping her mom in the kitchen.

**6. D:** Too much milk would make the cookie mix runny like soup.

## Mr. Smith and the Garden

**1. C:** This story is mainly about Mr. Smith planting seeds in his garden.

**2. D:** Mr. Smith bought his seeds at the store.

**3. B:** Mr. Smith planted carrot seeds and lettuce seeds.

**4. A:** Mr. Smith will eat the lettuce and carrots in salads.

## Pedro and the Zoo

**1. C:** Pedro was happy about going to the zoo.

**2. B:** Pedro was mad when his mom said to clean his room.

**3. B:** Pedro was glad because he got to go to the zoo after he cleaned his room.

**4. D:** Pedro learned that chores must be done before having fun.

**5. D:** Pedro's dad said "chores come before fun."

## Ashley and the Circus

**1. C:** The story took place at a circus.

**2. D:** The story took place at night.

**3. B:** We know it was a circus because there were clowns and a lion tamer there.

**4. A:** We know it was at night because it was past Ashley's bedtime.

## Ray's Story

**1.** new

**2.** dog

**3.** three

**4.** piggy bank

**5.** happy

## Emma's Day Off

**1.** 5

**2.** 1

**3.** 2

**4.** 4

**5.** 3

# Reading: Foundational Skills

## Long A and Short A

1. hat; Short

2. tape; Long

3. cat; Short

4. cake; Long

5. ant; Short

## Long E and Short E

1. deer; Long

2. wheel; Long

3. egg; Short

4. bee; Long

5. bed; Short

## Long I and Short I

1. kite; Long

2. tire; Long

3. bird; Short

4. pig; Short

5. pin; Short

## Long O and Short O

1. dog; Short

2. log; Short

3. rope; Long

4. soap; Long

5. mop; Short

## Long U and Short U

1. cube; Long

2. butter; Short

3. tub; Short

4. cup; Short

5. sun; Short

### BL, BR, FL, FR

1. blue

2. black or brown

3. flower

4. fly

5. frown

6. bread

7. brain

8. floating

### CL, CR, CH, WH

1. white

2. church

3. crown

4. clock

5. clown

6. cross

7. chips

8. whale

**GL, PL, SL**

1. slide
2. plug
3. plate
4. gloves
5. globe
6. sled

**TH, TR, GR**

1. train
2. grapes
3. tree
4. gravy
5. thumb
6. thirty

**SH, SK, ST**

1. shoes
2. sheep
3. skating
4. sky
5. steak
6. states

**SM, SN, SP**

1. smile
2. snails
3. snakes
4. spots
5. sponge

**-SH, -CH, -ND, -CK**

1. wash
2. pond
3. sand
4. lunch
5. duck
6. truck
7. watch
8. fish

**-NT, -MP, -NK, -ST**

1. ant
2. stamp
3. bank
4. nest
5. skunk
6. lamp
7. toast
8. tent

## What Rhymes With It?

1. bat - cat
2. frog - dog
3. more - store
4. far - car
5. soap - rope

## What Is It?

1. glass
2. bike
3. snake
4. cow
5. cat
6. fish
7. duck
8. hat
9. kite

## Words That End With an "E"

1. hose
2. rode
3. bake
4. flake
5. grace
6. ripe
7. grape
8. bike
9. score
10. rose

## Common Long Vowel Combinations

1. oa = coal

2. ee = feet

3. ee = deer

4. ea = eat

5. ea = squeak

6. ie = tie

7. ui = suit

8. ui = fruit

9. ai = raining

10. ai = paint

## How Many Syllables?

1. frog = 1

2. house = 1

3. pony = 2

4. elephant = 3

5. cat = 1

6. teacher = 2

7. basketball = 3

8. strawberry = 3

9. airplane = 2

10. dog = 1

## Let's Break It Up!

1. mail-man

2. foot-ball

3. ham-mer

4.ov-en

5. rain-ing

6. prob-lem

7. mon-ey

8. wom-an

9. cit-y

10. sev-en

## Comprehension and Recognition

**1. C:** school bus

**2. C:** duck

**3. D:** house

## Word Recognition

**1. B:** puppy

**2. A:** cow

**3. A:** new

**4. C:** frown

## Identifying Sounds at the Beginning of Words

**1. A:** cat

**2. C:** dog

**3. D:** top

**4. C:** move

# Reading: Language

## Nouns

1. rope

2. lake

3. turtle

4. car

5. book

6. hat

7. face

8. fruit

9. dime

10. ball

## Proper Nouns

1. Jane

2. Mr. Martinez

3. President Obama

4. Empire State Building

5. Grandpa

6. Doctor Harris

7. Smoky Bear

8. Atlanta Braves

9. Easter

10. Fluffy

## Possessive Nouns

**1. B:** Billy's baseball bat

**2. A:** the cats' food dishes

**3. A:** my dad's car

**4. B:** my grandparents' house

**5. C:** the blender's noise

**6. A:** the flowers' aroma

**7. A:** my friend's sister

**8. C:** my friends' sisters

**9. C:** my dog's collar

**10. C:** the teacher's desk

## Personal Pronouns

**1. C:** He

**2. A:** They

**3. D:** he

**4. B:** I

**5. D:** it

**6. C:** him

**7. D:** you

**8. A:** we

**9. B:** us

**10. A:** they

## Possessive Pronouns

**1. C:** their

**2. A:** your

**3. C:** its

**4. B:** his

**5. A:** her

## Indefinite Pronouns

1. None

2. anything

3. Most

4. several

5. anybody

6. either

7. others

8. everything

9. both

10. some

## Verbs

1. run

2. walk

3. talk

4. kick

5. send

6. drive

7. bake

8. throw

9. freeze

10. put

## Subject-Verb Agreement

**1. C:** rides

**2. A:** ride

**3. B:** live

**4. A:** lives

**5. C:** is

**6. B:** are

**7. B:** help

**8. C:** helps

**9. B:** bakes

**10. A:** bake

## Verb Tenses

1.
   a. FUTURE
   b. PRESENT
   c. PAST
2.
   a. PRESENT
   b. FUTURE
   c. PAST
3.
   a. PAST
   b. FUTURE
   c. PRESENT
4.
   a. FUTURE
   b. PRESENT
   c. PAST
5.
   a. PAST
   b. FUTURE
   c. PRESENT

## ADJECTIVES

**1.**

a. new is the adjective
b. puppy is the noun

**2.**

a. chubby is the adjective
b. baby is the noun

**3.**

a. fun is the adjective
b. Recess is the noun

**4.**

a. loud is the adjective
b. alarm is the noun

**5.**

a. happy is the adjective
b. Amber is the noun

## CONJUNCTIONS

1. for

2. or

3. but

4. so

5. and

## DETERMINERS

1. a

2. this

3. that

4. These

5. those

### Prepositions

**1. D:** Mrs. Gonzales is the name OF my teacher.

**2. C:** This ball belongs TO Ramona.

**3. B:** I like jelly ON my toast.

**4. D:** Let's run TO the park.

**5. D:** Juan is FROM Dallas, Texas.

### Rule 1: First Word in a Sentence

1. A bear can sleep all winter.

2. Boys and girls both like playing at recess.

3. Chess is a fun game that makes you think ahead.

4. Don't forget your umbrella!

5. Eating too much candy can make you sick.

6. Frogs like to eat flies and other bugs

7. Going to Sea World last year was my best trip ever.

8. How long does it take for cookies to bake?

9. It rained all day yesterday.

10. Joining Boy Scouts is one of the best things I ever did.

11. Keeping up with homework is easy if you do it before you go out and play.

12. Let's go see what Mom is making for supper.

13. My uncle is a park ranger and works every day in the forest.

14. Now I'm going to do a magic trick.

15. Painting can be fun, but it can be messy, too.

16. Reading books is one of the best ways to spend your spare time.

17. Quiet, please; it's time to begin.

18. Six plus two equals eight.

19. Taking a bath every night keeps us clean.

20. You should always look both ways before crossing a street.

## Rule 2: Pronoun "I"

1. When it rains I will get wet if I forget my umbrella.

2. I really enjoy playing baseball.

3 My cat purrs when I pet her.

4. My dog will sit up and beg when I give him a treat.

5. When school is called off after it snows, I enjoy sleeping late.

6. Today I found a quarter on the sidewalk.

7. If my parents say it's OK, I want you to come over this Saturday.

8. Going to the dentist is something I don't enjoy.

9. If you will help me with my homework, I will help you do the dishes.

10. I helped mom make breakfast in bed for Dad on Father's Day.

11. We found a stray kitten yesterday, and I helped feed it with a bottle.

12. On September 27th, I will turn seven years old.

13. When school is out for the summer, I will be going to North Dakota to visit my grandparents.

14. Every night before I go to sleep, my parents pray with me and then tuck me in.

15. When I grow up I want to be a firefighter.

16. My piggy bank is getting full, so I will empty it soon and count my money.

17. Last week I scored a run for my Little League team.

18. On Fridays I like to ride my bike to school.

19. If Dad takes the new job, I will be moving to Indiana.

20. Mom told me I need a haircut.

## Rule 3: Proper Nouns

1. Dad and I went to a new grocery store called Hanover's.

*"Dad" is your father's title, and it's the first word of the sentence. "Hanover's" is the name of a store.*

2. I asked Mrs. Benson if I could have more mashed potatoes.

*"Mrs. Benson" is a person's name.*

3. Our parents got us two kittens, and Lateesha and I named them Fluffy and Tiger.

*"Lateesha" is the proper name of the sister, and "Fluffy" and "Tiger" are the proper names of the kittens.*

4. My favorite football team is the Dallas Cowboys.

*"Dallas Cowboys" is the proper name of a football team.*

5. Last week Doctor Smith said I will need braces.

*"Doctor Smith" is the title of a dentist.*

6. Our new priest is Father Rodriguez.

*"Father Rodriguez" is the title of a priest.*

7. We're having a birthday party for Uncle Bob tonight.

*"Uncle Bob" is a title.*

8. On Sunday we have lunch with Grandma and Grandpa after church.

*"Grandma" and "Grandpa" are titles.*

9. Did Mom talk to your parents about the slumber party?

*"Mom" is a title*

10. I have a sister named Joan, but we all call her Cissy.

*"Joan" is the name of the sister, and "Cissy" is her nickname.*

## Rule 4: Places

1. My friend Pierre moved here from Canada.

*Canada is a country*

2. Tommy plays soccer at rogers park on the weekends.

*Rogers Park is the name of a park*

3. There are over a hundred nations in Africa.

*Africa is a continent*

4. Last year, we visited the Empire State Building.

*The Empire State Building is the official name of a building.*

5. The Chicago Cubs play their home games at Wrigley Field.

*Wrigley Field is the name of a baseball stadium.*

6. My cousin lives in Fargo, North Dakota.

*Fargo is a city, and North Dakota is a state.*

7. My mom and dad are going to take our family on a trip to paris, france, next year.

*Paris is a city, and France is a country.*

8. I want to be the first human to walk on Mars.

*Mars is a planet.*

9. My aunt and uncle live in a huge house in Atlanta.

*Atlanta is a city.*

10. The city of Chicago, Illinois, is located in Cook County.

*Chicago is a city, Illinois is a state, and Cook County is a county.*

## Rule 5: Dates

1. December 25th

2. January 1st

3. Monday

4. Friday

5. November

## More Capitalization Questions

1. Today is Monday.

*Today is the first word of the sentence. Monday is a day of the week.*

2. I will be seven years old on June 1st.

*The personal pronoun I should always be capitalized. June is a month.*

3. My friend Sally is wearing a blue dress.

*Sally is the name of a person.*

4. Don't miss out on the Christmas light show.

*Christmas is a holiday*

5. I went with my dad to Burger Town for lunch on Saturday.

*Burger Town is the name of a business. Saturday is a day of the week. The word "dad" is not capitalized because it is not a proper noun. (If the sentence said "I went with my Dad to Burger Town for lunch on Saturday", then Dad would be capitalized, because it becomes a title.)*

6. My cat's name is Bonnie.

*Bonnie is the name of a pet.*

7. For Thanksgiving we are going to Dallas to visit my grandparents.

*For is the first word of the sentence. Thanksgiving is a holiday. Dallas is a city. The word "grandparents" is not capitalized because it is a common noun, not a title or form of address.*

8. How are you today, Grandma?

*Grandma is a title or form of address*

9. Mr. Smith is wearing a blue suit.

*Mr. Smith is a person's title.*

10. Is it time for lunch yet, Billy?

*Billy is a person's name.*

11. In church, Reverend Biggs told us a Bible story.

*Reverend Biggs is the title of a church leader, used as a form of address. The Bible is a sacred religious book.*

12. Principal Jones is also the baseball coach.

*Principal Jones is a form of address, but "the baseball coach" is not.*

13. Coach Jones is also the school principal.

*Coach Jones is a form of address, but "the school principal" is not.*

14. Aunt Sally is coming over for Sunday dinner.

*Aunt Sally is a form of address. Sunday is a day of the week.*

15. On Sunday my aunt is coming over for dinner.

*Sunday is a day of the week. The phrase "my aunt" is not a form of address, or title, so it should not be capitalized.*

16. My mom went to a college in Ohio.

*Ohio is a state. The phrase "my mom" is not a form of address, and "a college" is not a specific place or name, so these phrases should not be capitalized.*

17. Dad went to Wabash College in Indiana.

*Dad is a form of address, and Wabash College is the name of a college, and Indiana is a state.*

18. The capital of Kentucky is Frankfort.

*Kentucky is a state, and Frankfort is a city.*

19. There are six flags in the parking lot.

*There is the first word of a sentence.*

20. I like going to Six Flags, the amusement park.

*Six Flags is the proper name of the amusement park.*

21. Our teacher is reading a book called My Friend Flicka to us.

*My Friend Flicka is the name of a book.*

22. At first, there were only 13 states in the United States of America.

*United States of America is the name of a country.*

23. We go to church almost every Sunday.

*We is the first word in the sentence. Sunday is a day of the week.*

24. We attend Morning Valley Baptist Church.

*Morning Valley Baptist Church is the name of a church.*

25. I gave Dad a present for Father's Day.

*Dad is a form of address, and Father's Day is a holiday*

## Punctuation

**1. A:** This sentence makes an ordinary statement, so it needs a period.

**2. B:** This sentence is asking a question, so it needs a question mark.

**3. A:** This is a simple statement, so it needs a period.

**4. C:** The speaker wants his dog to know how much he loves him, so he uses exaggeration to get his message across. This kind of sentence needs an exclamation point.

**5. B:** This is a question, so it needs a question mark.

**6. C:** This is not a statement, and it's not a question. It's an expression of strong emotion, so it needs an exclamation point.

**7. C:** This is not a statement, and it's not a question. It's an expression of strong emotion, so it needs an exclamation point.

**8. A:** This is a statement about a question, so it might be confusing. But even though the sentence is about a question, it is still a statement, so it needs a period.

**9. A:** This is a statement, so it needs a period.

**10. B:** This is a question, so it needs a question mark.

## Rule 1: Use Commas With a List

1. I ride to school with Cindy, Bob, LaShawn, and Manny.

2. The names of the flowers are tulips, roses, daffodils, and lilies.

3. Joe, Mark, and Greg are the tallest boys in the class.

4. I like football, baseball, soccer, and basketball.

5. Red, blue, and yellow are her favorite colors.

## Rule 2: Use Commas Between Cities And States

1. Houston, Texas

2. Akron, Ohio

3 New York, New York

4. Nashville, Tennessee

5. Salt Lake City, Utah

## Rule 3: Use Commas In Dates

1. March 15, 1985

2. June 2, 2022

3. July 10, 1959

4. October 30, 1492

5. August 15, 1979

## Letter Practice

1. A and a for apple

2. Z and z for zebra

3. M and m for mouse

4. K and k for kangaroo

5. E and e for ear

6. N and n for nose

7. B and b for baseball/G and g for glove

8. C and c for cat

9. D and d for dog

10. U and u for umbrella

11. H and h for house

12. G and g for girl

13. R and r for rope

14. P and p for pie

15. X and x for x-ray

16. J and j for jar

17. Q and q for queen

18. S and s for sun

19. T and t for tiger

20. W and w for window

21. F and f for fan

22. Y and y for yawn

23. L and l for lion

24. V and v for vine

25. O and o for owl

26. I and I for iron

## Same Word, Different Meanings

1. watch

2. park

3. light

4. sign

5. fall

6. foot

7. change

8. sink

9. roll

10. trip

## Prefixes and Suffixes

**1. D:** writer

**2. B:** preschool

**3. B:** unbuckle

**4. A:** happier

**5. D:** weekly

# Answers and Explanations for Test #1

**1. A:** Julie's brother is telling this story. She calls her brother "Bill" during the story. This shows that Bill is telling the story.

**2. D:** Look back at the story to remember its details. The second sentence is "We got there before noon."

**3. B:** Julie and her brother have trouble getting used to the cold water. But he tells her to "be patient. We might get used to the cold." Julie learns that being patient is good because this is how she gets used to the cold water.

**4. A:** Putting on the play was Karen's idea. Rudy says it is a great idea. Since all the adults have fun watching the play, we know that it really was a good idea. This shows that Karen has good ideas.

**5. C:** Books are a lot longer than stories. We do not know if it would be funnier, so choice A is wrong. We don't know if it would be more serious or less interesting either. So choices B and D are wrong too.

**6. B:** The whole story is about how cats are good pets. They like to rub against people. They are good at telling people what they want. They do not take up much of people's time. Based on these clues, you can guess that <u>wonderful</u> means <u>very good</u>.

**7. C:** The story says, "Sometimes cats like to be left alone, so they will not take up a lot of your time." Some cats sleep 16 hours a day, but not every cat does this. So choice A is wrong. Cats meow and purr, which are sounds. This means they are not totally silent and choice B is wrong. Choice D is wrong because the story is about how a lot of cats like people.

**8. D:** The second sentence of the story gives the answer to this question. It says, "Like dogs, they can be very loving." Only cats purr and meow, so choices C and D are wrong.

**9. C:** This story is all about the guitar. Do not let the title confuse you. The "Singing Strings" are not real singers. They are the guitar strings that sound like they are singing because they make music.

**10. A:** The story "Singing Strings" does not say anything about violins. The story says that guitars have strings, so choice B is wrong. It also says these strings can be plucked, so choice C is wrong too.

**11. B:** <u>The</u> is the first word of the sentence. The first word of a sentence should always start with an uppercase letter. So the letter <u>T</u> in <u>The</u> should be uppercase in this sentence.

**12. D:** Both <u>me</u> and <u>see</u> have a long <u>e</u> sound. The <u>e</u> in <u>pet</u> is a short sound, so choice B is wrong. The <u>e</u> in <u>men</u> is a short sound too, so choice C is wrong. Choice A is wrong because the <u>e</u> in <u>the</u> is silent.

**13. C:** The words <u>from</u> and <u>frog</u> have the same first sound. They both start with a blend of the letters <u>f</u> and <u>r</u>.

**14. A:** Choice A is the right way to spell the color <u>blue</u>. The letters <u>ue</u> make an "oo" sound.

**15. B:** In the sentence, the bug sits on a person's finger. Fingers are small. That means a bug would have to be small to sit on a finger. These clues help you to know what <u>tiny</u> means. It means <u>very small</u>.

**16. A:** This is the right way to spell the word. The letters <u>ai</u> do not always make an "eh" sound, but they do in <u>again</u>.

**17. D:** The word <u>sign</u> may look like it is spelled wrong. That is because it does not have a g sound. But the g is silent. This is the right way to spell <u>sign</u>.

**18. B:** The <u>a</u> in <u>baby</u> has a long vowel sound. It does not need to be blended with a <u>y</u>. So choice A is wrong. It does not need an extra <u>a</u>, so choice C is wrong too. The <u>a</u> does not need to be blended with an <u>e</u>, so choice D is also wrong.

**19. A:** The story should be about how you feel about a sport. The only title that fits is "Baseball Is the Best." It shows that you think baseball is the best sport. The other titles do not show how you feel.

**20. C:** Choice A is right because it is the only one in the right order. You would not go to school while you are sitting in class. You would go to school before sitting in class. So choice A is wrong. Choices B and D are out of order too.

**21. D:** Computers can be used to write stories. The other answer choices are tools that are not used for writing.

**22. B:** Sometimes you have to do reading to be able to answer a question in a story. Sometimes you can use things from your own life to write it. A story about what you did yesterday would just come from your own life. You would not have to do any reading to write it.

**23. D:** There are rules for talking in class. Choices A, B, and C all break these rules. Only choice D is a good thing to do during a lesson.

**24. A:** Sometimes your teacher will teach things you do not understand at first. That is normal, but make sure you ask your teacher to explain it again. This way you will not fall behind the rest of your class.

**25. B:** Only choice B is a clear way to talk about your grandfather. Choice A repeats information. Choice C does not say what your grandfather likes clearly. Choice D is not a complete sentence.

**26. C:** Choice C is the best answer because it shows a picture of a fish. This helps a story about fish because it shows how they look. The other answer choices do not show pictures of fish.

**27. B:** The first word of a sentence should start with an uppercase letter. People's names should start with uppercase letters, too. Only choice B has the right letters written in the upper case.

**28. D:** When the subject of a sentence is just one thing, the verb should end with an s. The subject of this sentence is girl. A girl is just one thing. So the verb run should have an s. Only choice D is right.

**29. A:** The verb read shows something that happened in the past. Yesterday happened in the past. So choice A is right. Tomorrow, next week, and next month have not happened yet. So choices B, C, and D are wrong.

**30. C:** The word and is the right way to join the cat and the dog in this sentence. It shows that they are doing something together.

**31. D:** The word over shows that something happened above something else. A bird flies above people.

**32. B:** The name of a month should start with an uppercase letter. The word May is a month in this sentence. So it should start with an uppercase M. Only answer choice B does this.

**33. B:** This sentence shows a list of things. There should be commas after every item in a list before the word and. Only choice B does this right.

**34. A:** Remember that g sometimes has a j sound. This will help you figure out that giraffe is the right spelling.

**35. C:** There is a clue in this word. The letters un are used to show an opposite. So unhappy means the opposite of happy. The opposite of happy is not happy.

**36. D:** This is a list of colors. Choice D, yellow, is the only answer that is a color.

**37. A:** A boat is used for sailing. Choices B, C, and D are things a boat cannot do.

**38. B:** Please is the only answer choice that makes sense in this sentence.

# Answers and Explanations for Test #2

**1. A:** Think about how the word whoosh sounds. Does it sound like wind zipping by? The writer uses whoosh to make you feel the speed of the sleds.

**2. D:** Think about what Jill says when she gets to the park. She says, "There were many nice hills there, all smooth with fresh snow." This shows that the park was snowy.

**3. B:** Jill's mom seems just as excited to sled as Jill is. So you can guess that they both like sledding. Only Jill is sleepy in this story. So choice A is wrong. Jill's mom is an adult, not a little girl. So choice C is wrong. The story does not say that Jill is an adult. If she is a child, she cannot drive a car. So choice D is wrong.

**4. C:** The first thing Sammy does on the farm is feed the chickens. Only after that does he go to the field and help his grandma plant corn. So choices A and B are wrong. Choice D is wrong because Sammy does not dig a hole, his grandma does.

**5. A:** Sammy sees his grandma digging in dirt in the field. The corn has not grown yet, so choice B is wrong. The story does not say anything about hills or paths. So choices C and D are wrong too.

**6. C:** Dragons and mermaids are not real. If you can paint things that are not real, then you can paint anything you can imagine.

**7. D:** This story gives directions on how to make a painting. It shows what you will need. It helps you think of things to paint. It tells you what to do when you are done painting.

**8. B:** Read the end of the story again. The writer says, "You did something that should make you feel proud. You just made art!" This shows that you should feel proud because you made art.

**9. B:** Choice B is the only right answer. Chapter 2 is called "What Monkeys Eat."

**10. A:** The monkey in the picture has a tail. None of the chapters say anything about monkey tails. So the only way to know that monkeys have tails is from the picture.

**11. C:** The o in owl has the same sound as the o in cow.

**12. D:** If you sound out lamb, it will sound like la-mm. The other answer choices would not sound like lamb if you said them out loud.

**13. A:** The letters oa form a long vowel sound that sounds like o.

**14. C:** A knife is a tool for cutting.

**15. D:** The exclamation point shows that this sentence should be read loudly. It is an exciting point in the story. Reading it loudly makes it more exciting!

**16. B:** This sentence is a question. A question should end with a question mark. Only choice B ends with a question mark.

**17. A:** In the word ear, the letters ea make an ee sound.

**18. B:** Use the sentence to help you find out what gnaw means. What do dogs do with bones? They chew them. So gnaw means chew.

**19. D:** "Playing the Piano" is a good title for a story telling how to play the piano. "Who Made the Piano?" sounds like a story about the person who invented the piano. So choice A is wrong. Choice B is wrong because it is the title of a story about people who play the piano. Choice C does not even say anything about the piano.

**20. C:** Learning about a subject before writing a story is called research. A good way to research birds is to read a book about them. Choices A, B, and D are not good ways to do research.

**21. B:** Choice B is right because it is the only one in the right order. The sun does not set after the stars shine. The sun sets first. So choice A is wrong. Choices B and D are out of order too.

**22. C:** Sometimes you have to do reading to be able to answer a question in a story. Sometimes you can use things from your own life to write it. A story about your favorite movie would just come from your own life. You would not have to do any reading to write it.

**23. D:** When your teacher asks you a question, you should answer it. Talk about a book if your teacher asks you about it. The teacher is not asking about lunch, so choice A is wrong. Choice C is wrong because the teacher is not asking about football.

**24. C:** This question asks you to imagine your friend is talking about books. To keep the talk going, you should also talk about books. Choice C is the only answer that stays on this subject.

**25. A:** It is important to understand class lessons well. Answer choices B, C, and D change the subject. They are not questions about the lesson. If you asked your teacher to explain the lesson again, you may understand it better. So choice A is the best answer.

**26. D:** Only choice D is a clear way to say what you learned from a book. Choices A, B, and C are not a complete sentences.

**27. B:** To show a word has something, end it with 's. Brian has the toy. So his name should be written Brian's in this sentence.

**28. A:** The word my shows that you have something. You have Gail as your best friend. So my is the right word to use in this sentence.

**29. C:** Adjectives are words that tell you more about something. This sentence needs an adjective that tells you what a raccoon's tail is like. A raccoon's tail is not slow, bad, or loud. It is furry.

**30. A:** The word an is used before a word that begins with the letter a and is only one thing. The word apple begins with an a. It is only one thing. So an is the best word for this sentence.

**31. D:** Sentences that tell someone to do something should end with a period. Choice A is wrong because it ends with a question mark. Choices B and C are not complete sentences.

**32. B:** An exclamation point shows excitement. Having the best day of your life is pretty exciting. So this sentence should end with an exclamation point.

**33. C:** The letters ch sometimes make a k sound. Echo is the right way to spell this word.

**34. D:** Think about how the word remain is used in the sentence. Fred is going to the beach. Petra is not. She is staying at home. The word remain means stay.

**35. B:** The word am shows that something is happening right now. A verb that is happening now ends with ing. So the correct word is thinking.

**36. A:** The sentence tells you that a swan can fly and swim. What kind of animal flies? A bird flies. So a swan is a bird that swims.

**37. C:** A mountain is not just big. It is very, very big. The word huge means very, very big. So C is the best answer choice.

**38. B:** This is a list of numbers. Two is a number. It is the only answer choice that belongs on this list.

## Online Resources

Due to our efforts to try to keep this book to a manageable length, we've created a link that will give you access to all of your online resources:

mometrix.com/resources719/ssterrag1rlwb

# It's Your Moment, Let's Celebrate It!

Share your story @mometrixtestpreparation